# 日常生活与"世纪末"的文学想象：
# 薇拉·凯瑟主要作品研究

*Rethinking Willa Cather's Everyday Life against the Fin-de-siècle Literary Imagination*

姜玲娣 ◎ 著

图书在版编目(CIP)数据

日常生活与"世纪末"的文学想象:薇拉·凯瑟主要作品研究/姜玲娣著.—合肥:安徽大学出版社,2021.6
ISBN 978-7-5664-2246-0

Ⅰ.①日… Ⅱ.①姜… Ⅲ.①薇拉·凯瑟—文学研究—英文 Ⅳ.①I712.065

中国版本图书馆 CIP 数据核字(2021)第 117275 号

# 日常生活与"世纪末"的文学想象:薇拉·凯瑟主要作品研究　　姜玲娣 著

| | |
|---|---|
| 出版发行: | 北京师范大学出版集团 |
| | 安 徽 大 学 出 版 社 |
| | (安徽省合肥市肥西路 3 号 邮编 230039) |
| | www.bnupg.com.cn |
| | www.ahupress.com.cn |
| 印　　刷: | 安徽利民印务有限公司 |
| 经　　销: | 全国新华书店 |
| 开　　本: | 170 mm×230 mm |
| 印　　张: | 10.25 |
| 字　　数: | 178 千字 |
| 版　　次: | 2021 年 6 月第 1 版 |
| 印　　次: | 2021 年 6 月第 1 次印刷 |
| 定　　价: | 35.00 元 |

ISBN 978-7-5664-2246-0

| | | | |
|---|---|---|---|
| 策划编辑:李　梅　李　雪 | | 装帧设计:李　军 | |
| 责任编辑:高婷婷　李　雪 | | 美术编辑:丁　健 | |
| 责任校对:韦　玮 | | 责任印制:赵明炎 | |

## 版权所有　　侵权必究

反盗版、侵权举报电话:0551—65106311
外埠邮购电话:0551—65107716
本书如有印装质量问题,请与印制管理部联系调换。
印制管理部电话:0551—65106311

# 前　言

薇拉·凯瑟（1873-1947）是美国20世纪上半叶著名的女作家。近年来，随着文学理论多元化趋势的加强，凯瑟研究亦呈现多元化的特征。其中，文化批评视角成为近十年来凯瑟研究的主流，凯瑟与现代文化之间的互动也成为评论界关注的焦点。然而，无论凯瑟与现代文化之间的互动有多么密切，一个不容忽视的事实就是，凯瑟善于从不同的文学传统中汲取精华，进而形成自己的创作美学。纵观其创作生涯，凯瑟从未停止在文学形式上的创新实验。尽管她的每一部新作都以不同的历史语境为背景，但她一直保持对"日常生活"实践活动的偏爱，尤其体现在"居住""烹饪""讲故事"等方面。

本书旨在探讨凯瑟日常生活美学在作品中的具体再现。日常生活为研究凯瑟的创作美学提供了一个很好的范式，因为这一研究不仅囊括凯瑟评论家们所关注的主要议题，而且有助于理解贯穿凯瑟整个创作生涯的创作主题和艺术追求。日常生活就像一面"棱镜"，透过它，读者可以蠡测凯瑟的创作美学观，即可审视凯瑟如何将自己的创作与地域文化、性别观念和现代意识联系在一起。

要理解凯瑟的日常生活美学，凯瑟作为"世纪末"转型时期的作家身份至关重要。换言之，凯瑟与"世纪末"文学想象的关系是理解凯瑟日常生活美学的一个关键因素。然而，仅梳理作家所生活的历史时代对其创作实践的影响还不足够。要对凯瑟的日常生活美学有一个全面而深入的理解，就必须找到有力的理论支撑。米歇尔·德塞都对日常生活与"讲故事"艺术的关系的论述、埃尔·梅约尔和吕斯·贾尔对"居住区""烹饪"的阐释都为本书的撰写提供了有力的理论支撑。

凯瑟的主要代表作品均以她童年时代的家乡——内不拉斯加的红云镇为原型。居住区在其创作中反复凸显，生动地再现了某种日常生活：借描绘家庭生活场景表现家中的权力分配；借居住区的地理布局来表现该居住区内不同阶级和族裔之间的相互关系；借"崖居人村"的遗迹追述已逝的印第安文明，表达这些古老的生活方式对现代人所施加的影响。凯瑟对"烹饪"的关注蕴含了她的多个创作主旨。在凯瑟的作品中，一方面，"烹饪"被提升到艺术的高度，无名的家庭主妇也因此成为凯瑟眼中的"艺术家"。另一方面，凯瑟打破了对"烹饪"这一活动的传统"性别"认知，塑造了勇于摆脱家庭束缚的"新女性"和热衷家庭生活的"新男性"形象。凯瑟的创作深受"口头叙事"文学的影响，其中一个突出表现是她在小说创作中热衷"插曲式"故事。在《死神来迎大主教》中，"讲故事"既是凯瑟的叙述方式，也是她的创作主题。凯瑟作品中众多的"插曲式"故事来源丰富，体裁多样，一个共同之处就是这些故事多讲述人类日常生活经验中阴暗的一面，如"痛苦""恐惧"和"死亡"。

本书分别从地理、性别和艺术三个不同维度对凯瑟文本中的日常生活进行讨论，旨在彰显凯瑟日常生活美学的复杂性。凯瑟的日常生活美学看似在描摹日常，但都能超越日常的琐碎和平凡。凯瑟对日常生活实践细节，如"居住""烹饪"的描写，并非只是单纯的记录或阐释，其中包含丰富的文化内涵和政治寓意。在凯瑟的大部分作品中，日常生活的客观事实得以浪漫化处理，她出色地将日常生活经验转化为艺术。

本书的撰写是基于本人的博士论文。本书从选题、构思到语言润色都受到导师杨金才教授的精心指导。本书的出版受到了南京邮电大学校级引进人才项目"日常生活与文学想象：薇拉·凯瑟主要作品研究"（校20190087）的资助。在本书出版过程中，安徽大学出版社的编辑仔细审阅了全书文稿，并帮助解决了各种难题。本人在此谨向各位老师表示衷心感谢。

由于本人水平有限，本书难免会有不足之处，恳请学界专家与读者给予指正。

姜玲娣<br>2021年6月

# Acknowledgements

I should like to express my deepest gratitude to all those who have made the publication of this book possible. I am especially indebted to my supervisor, Professor Yang Jincai, for initiating my interest in Willa Cather, for knocking me out of my smugness and narrow-mindedness and pushing me forward on this project. Without his encouragement and academic guidance, I could not have stuck to the end of this academic endeavor. I am also obliged to all my teachers throughout my MA and Ph.D studies in Nankai University and Nanjing University for their academic help both in and out of the classroom.

I am also grateful to Professor Mark Morrisson for his assistance as a contact advisor while I was studying at The Pennsylvania State University as a visiting Ph. D student. I should also thank Professor Cheryl Glenn for inviting me to her seminar and giving me valuable suggestions. In addition, I would like to acknowledge my indebtedness to Professor Jenna Mead at University of Western Australia for her insightful reading. I thank Professor Wang Yukuo of Nanjing University of Posts and Telecommunications for his encouragement and support all through the publication of this book.

I owe a great debt of gratitude to one young distinguished Cather scholar, Zhou Ming at Renmin University of China for sharing with me his collected materials on

Cather. I also want to extend my special thanks to my friends Xie Youguang, Cheng Zhaoxi and Fan Xiaohong for helping me collect materials for my book writing during their stay in the United States.

I would also like to acknowledge the funding of Nanjing University of Posts and Telecommunications. My thanks also goes to Anhui University Press for editing my book.

Finally, I owe an immeasurable debt to my parents, my husband, my two dear daughters and all my dear friends. Without their sustained love and support, this book could not have been completed.

# List of Abbreviations

ALL     *A Lost Lady* (1923)
DCA     *Death Comes for the Archbishop* (1927)
EN     *Early Novels* (1987)
KA     *The Kingdom of Art: Willa Cather's First Principles and Critical Statements, 1893-1896* (1966)
LN     *Later Novels* (1990)
MÁ     *My Ántonia* (1918)
MME     *My Mortal Enemy* (1926)
NR     "Neighbor Rosicky" (1932)
NS     *Novels and Stories* (1918)
OO     *One of Ours* (1922)
OP     *O Pioneers!* (1913)
PH     *The Professor's House* (1925)
SL     *The Song of the Lark* (1915)
SR     *Shadows on the Rock* (1931)
SSG     *Sapphira and the Slave Girl* (1940)
WCW     *Willa Cather on Writing: Critical Studies on Writing as an Art* (1949)
WP     *The World and the Parish: Willa Cather's Articles and Reviews, 1893-1902* (1970)

# Contents

**Chapter I   The Basics of Willa Cather Novels**..........................................................1

  1.1   A Random Reflection on Willa Cather............................................................1

  1.2   The Discussions on Willa Cather Novels........................................................3

**Chapter II   The Practice of the Neighborhood**........................................................37

  2.1   The Political Side of Domesticity in *Sapphira and the Slave Girl* ...............40

  2.2   Propriety and Sexuality in the Neighborhood of *Shadows on the Rock*

       and *A Lost Lady* ..........................................................................................50

  2.3   "Dead" Neighborhood in *The Song of the Lark* and *The Professor's House*...59

**Chapter III   Doing-cooking** ....................................................................................71

  3.1   The Gendered Aspect of Doing-cooking .......................................................72

  3.2   The Smells of the Past in "Neighbor Rosicky" and *My Ántonia* ................88

  3.3   The Cultural Aspect of Cather's Foodways ...................................................93

**Chapter IV  The Act of Storytelling** ....................................................................... 103

    4.1   Everyday Life Narration in *Death Comes for the Archbishop* ..................... 106

    4.2   The Art of Storytelling in *My Ántonia* ........................................................ 119

**Chapter V  Conclusion** ............................................................................................. 130

**Bibliography** .............................................................................................................. 137

# Chapter I
# The Basics of Willa Cather Novels

## 1.1 A Random Reflecion on Willa Cather

Literary debates on fiction in various periods tend to center on questions of representation: Who or what might be represented in fiction, in what manner, and by whom? For whom is the subject represented? In what sense can an author or a literary work be judged highbrow, middlebrow or lowbrow?[①] To what extent is aesthetic representation enmeshed with political representation, gender issues and ethnic otherness? Different answers to these questions may indicate diverse artistic principles upheld by individual authors. Yet it is often the case that there is no clear-cut distinction between one choice and another.

In the case of the American novelist Willa Cather, what she writes about is everyday activities; nevertheless, in her fiction, everyday activities, such as living and cooking, are often elevated to the status of art. Cather's rare ability to bridge the

---

[①] In the words of Lawrence W. Levine, from the time of their formulation, such cultural categories as highbrow and lowbrow were hardly meant to be neutral descriptive terms; they were openly associated with and designed to preserve, nurture, and extend the cultural history and values of a particular group of peoples in a specific historical context. Hence in applying them to evaluation of certain literary works or individual authors, the cultural history and the specific historical context during which the author lived must be taken into consideration.

gap between the highbrow and the middlebrow; and to keep the two in conversation, has long been acknowledged by scholars (Murphy, 2003: 270; Stout, 2012: 28). Yet, for the significance she gave to "the ritual of the ordered life and to the niceties of cookery" (Trilling, 1980: 65), Cather was regarded by Lionel Trilling as a defender of gentility and her writing quite similar to "the gaudy domesticity of bourgeois accumulation glorified in the *Woman's Home Companion*" (1980: 67). Similarly, Cather was accused by Granville Hicks of "political conservatism" for her failure to address in her works "what is central and fundamental in her own age" (qtd. in Schroeter, 1967: 140-144). Accusations such as Trilling's and Hicks's have been proven invalid in today's literary criticism since more and more scholars consider Cather an active participant in modern cultures, cautioning against interpreting her too narrowly or taking her words too literally (qtd. in Murphy, 1984: 23).

Born in the late-Victorian Period, Cather emerged at a critical moment when American culture was shifting to the Modernist Period. Cather began her apprenticeship while she was still in college, during which she not only read voraciously, but also contributed to or edited as many as five periodicals. After her graduation, Cather worked in the journalism for another thirteen years, rising to the position of managing editor of distinguished magazines such as the *Home Monthly* and *McClure's*. Her final break from journalism did not come until she encountered Sarah Orne Jewett in 1908. In her letter to Cather on December 13, Jewett prompted Cather to leave her job as an editor and to commit to full-time writing (1911: 247). Cather followed Jewett's suggestion and with it, she became a writer of several classic works. *O Pioneers!*, *The Song of the Lark*, *My Ántonia*, *A Lost Lady*, *The Professor's House* and *Death Comes for the Archbishop* compose a list of works that would be the envy of virtually any other twentieth-century novelist.

During her lifetime, Cather's literary reputation remained relatively steady until the publication of *One of Ours*. She was regarded as an excellent delineator of the landscape of Nebraska and a fine stylist. After an initial awkward imitation of the literary style of Henry James in her first short-story collection *The Troll Garden* and the novel *Alexander's Bridge*, she laid claim to her true subject and found her authentic voice in *O Pioneers!* (De Roche, 2006: 67). Critical responses to her other two novels, *The Song of the Lark* and *My Ántonia*, were equally enthusiastic. *My Ántonia* in particular has won much favor from critics. For instance, H. L. Mencken considered this novel a good indication of its author's "high artistic conscience", and he also called it "one of the best that any American has ever done" (qtd. in O'Connor, 2001: 88-89).

Cather's great success came with the appearance of *One of Ours*. The novel helped its author win the Pulitzer Prize, yet was the subject of numerous attacks. In Mencken's opinion, the war depicted in *One of Ours* was "fought out, not in France, but on a Hollywood movie-lot"; Edmund Wilson considered the novel "a pretty flat failure"; Sinclair Lewis deemed it inferior to other novels of Cather (Schroeter, 1967: 14-42). In a letter to Edmund Wilson, Ernest Hemingway wrote, "Look at *One of Ours*. Prize, big sale, people taking it seriously. You were in the war, weren't you? Wasn't that last scene in the lines wonderful? Do you know where it came from? The battle scene in *Birth of a Nation*[①]. I identified episode after episode. Catherized. Poor woman, she had to get her war experience somewhere." (qtd. in Wilson, 1952: 110) Whereas negative views of *One of Ours* from Mencken may have foretold Hicks's censorship of Cather's idealism several years later[②], Hemingway's remarks were clearly gender-biased. In other words, his explicit attack on Cather had much to do with the fact that as a woman writer, Cather should have dared to write about male experience.

## 1.2 The Discussions on Willa Cather Novels

Despite the high acclaim she received for her later 1920s novels like *A Lost Lady*, *The Professor's House* and *Death Comes for the Archbishop*, in the next decade, Cather's work nearly fell into oblivion as critics faulted her for being out of

---

① *Birth of a Nation* is a 1915 American silent drama film directed by D. W. Griffith and it chronicles the relationship of two families in Civil War and Reconstruction-US era. The film was a commercial success when it was released.

② In "The Case against Willa Cather", Granville Hicks wrote, "From the first, it is clear, the one theme that seemed to Miss Cather worth writing about was heroic idealism, the joyous struggle against nature sustained by a confidence in the ultimate beneficence of that nature against which it fought."

touch with the painful social and economic realities of the Depression-era. According to Paul R. Petrie, two of Cather's final three novels—*Sapphira and the Slave Girl* and *Shadows on the Rock* are set in the historical past[①], which provides Left Critics the perfect opportunity to reevaluate the Cather canon according to their own aesthetic (1996: 28). In the year of 1933 and 1937, Left Critics such as the above mentioned Hicks and Trilling issued the most damning indictments of Cather's works.

Hicks, for instance, made fun of Cather's "heroic idealism" and lamented the lack of "the robustness of a Dreiser or the persistence of an Anderson" in Cather's works (qtd. in Schroeter, 1967: 142-147). Trilling too felt irritated by Cather's exclusion of elements of modern life in her latest books and considered her "turn to the ideas of a vanished time" in these works a "weary response to weariness" (1980: 66-67). In a letter of April 1936 to *The Commonweal*, Cather responded to Hicks's attack by writing an essay titled "Escapism", arguing that an "escapist" tendency is inherent in art and should not be derogated. "Economics and art are strangers," she maintained, and thus art should not be devoted to propaganda for economic or social reform (*WCW* 27). Despite her efforts to win back the battle, Cather's clarification was useless and her refutation failed to find an echo in the 1930s.

Trilling's criticism of Cather was of course for good reason and his judgment was an outcome of the literary and social contexts of his age. The same year that Trilling argued against the "spirituality" of Cather's latest books, citing her "exclusion of those elements of modern life" and her disregard of "the social and political facts" (1980: 66), John Steinbeck published his novella *Of Mice and Men*, with his Pulitzer Prize-winning novel *The Grapes of Wrath* followed two years later—both of which were set against the Great Depression. American literature in the 1930s also witnessed the publication of John Dos Passos's *U. S. A. Trilogy* (*The 42nd*

---

① Cather's *Death Comes for the Archbishop* is based on historical record and features historical persons, thus it could also be regarded as a historical novel. It is interesting to notice the sharp contrast in critical reactions that had been caused by the publication of *Death Comes for the Archbishop* and two of Cather's later fictions. Unlike the negative views the latter had got, critical consensus about *Death Comes for the Archbishop* was favorable and even enthusiastic. Such differences can be an indication of the powerful impact of social atmosphere on literary criticism.

*Parallel, 1919* and *The Big Money*) in 1930, 1932 and 1936, all of which focused on the historical development of American society during the first three decades of the twentieth century. Compared with these up-to-date works, Cather's fiction appears to be out of date.

In addition, in the words of Reynolds, in finding faults with Cather's depiction of the domestic interior culture, Trilling actually inherited the American male literary tradition. Prior to his criticism of Cather was Nathaniel Hawthorne's bitter comment about the "scribbling women", Henry James's complaints in the voice of Basil Ransom in *The Bostonians* about "the whole generation is womanized", and Van Wyck Brooks's accusation of the American intellect of being ruined by "feminization" (qtd. in Reynolds, 1996: 37-40). Taking these male predecessors' remarks into account, it is no wonder that Trilling articulated such harsh criticism against Cather.

Negative reviews incurred by the publication of *One of Ours* along with the biting remarks from the Left Critics exerted great influence on the reception of Cather's works in the following decades. The 1930s marked a turning point in Cather scholarship. As James Schroeter has observed, "For the first time a crack appeared in the critical façade. To be sure, the crack was only a minority report; but what made it ominous was that... it mounted a full-scale attack not only on Miss Cather's new work but on the direction of her entire career." (1967: 135) When she died in April 1947, the obituary printed in the most influential newspaper and magazines of the day still carried the tone of the 1930s. For instance, the obituary in the *Nation* gave only a brief introduction to Cather's accomplishments, saying wearily that she was a minor novelist, "remote from... the problems of the last two anxious decades" (qtd. in Zabel, 1974: 713).[1]

Cather criticism of the fifties and sixties was less sensational than that of the

---

[1] The obituary in the *New York Times* involved a brief account of the author's accomplishment and it conceded that like Theodore Dreiser, Sherwood Anderson and Sinclair Lewis, Cather helped mold the "American tradition" in literature. *The Times* admitted that she held an honored and significant place among the older generation of American novelists; however, it also contended that there was a certain imaginative slightness, an absence of depth or genuinely creative power in her works.

former decades. The major critical trend of the day, featured by a New Critical approach, stayed away from her for her prose did not possess the formal intricacies featured by New Criticism (Acocella, 2000: 32). Thanks to feminist critics' efforts to reconstruct a "female canon", Cather criticism revived in the 1970s. Cather's literary career as a self-supported female writer, as well as her creation of many strong-willed new women figures in her works, clearly help her draw the attention of the feminist literary critics. Yet feminist critics encountered some thorny problems when they tried to enlist Cather in their group. Cather's intimacy with many of her female friends in her personal life, her use of male narrators and the appearance of same-sex friendship in some of her works caused considerable controversy in the academia. Blanche Gelfant confronted the topic of Cather's handling of sex in his critical essay "The Forgotten Reaping-Hook: Sex in *My Ántonia*", in which he argued that "Jim Burden belongs to a remarkable gallery of characters for whom Cather consistently invalidates sex" (1971: 62). Following Gelfant's statement, Jane Rule, a Canadian novelist and critic, declared that Cather was homosexual in her 1975 book *Lesbian Images*. Rule's matter-of-fact declaration did not end but sharpened the debates over the sexual orientation of Cather (qtd. in Acocella, 2000: 43).

With the publication of Sharon O'Brien's *Willa Cather: The Emerging Voice* and Marilee Lindemann's *Willa Cather: Queering America*, Cather's status as a lesbian writer seemed to be finally settled. Yet today there remain a group of scholars who have some reservations about this topic. When interviewed about Cather's sexuality on the program "Willa Cather: The Road Is All"[1], Susan Rosowski responded, "we are so narrow in our definitions of 'love' " and Joan Acocella said, "We don't know Willa Cather and Isabella are lovers; indeed we don't know whether Cather ever has a lover; in the sense we 'define' them" (2000: 24). When *The Selected Letters of Willa Cather* came out in 2013, critics rushed to it for they wanted to find evidence for or against Cather's lesbianism. But Cather once again let them down. None of her letters to Isabelle McClung Hambourg (the Pittsburgh socialite widely considered the

---

[1] Featuring the life and career of author Willa Cather, "Willa Cather: The Road Is All" is one of the *American Masters* series program directed by Christine Lesiak and Joel Geyer. The program was aired on PBS on Wednesday, Sep. 7, 2005.

love of her life), or Edith Lewis (who is her companion and housemate for nearly 40 years) contain any shocking or revealing information.

Apart from studies revolving around the sexuality of the writer, topics of continuing interest to Cather scholars include the novelist's relation to other women writers and her conception of professional authorship as shaped by definitions of gender. Fearing that identification with women writers would threaten her status as a serious literary artist, Cather purposefully held herself aloof from her female predecessors and contemporaries. Against her initial wishes, nowadays, questions of influence and connection between Cather and other female writers draw much attention from critics. Comparisons and parallels are made between Cather's works and aesthetics and those of a great number of female writers, including Toni Morrison, Virginia Woolf, Edith Wharton, Katherine Anne Porter, Zora Neale Hurston, Dorothy Canfield Fisher, Eudora Welty and Ellen Glasgow, to name just a few.

Cather scholarship in the last two decades of the twentieth century continued the momentum of the 1970s when an exploration of New Critical perspectives enabled scholars to see her fiction operate on more levels than previously thought. Critical perspectives on Cather in the 1980s and 1990s included feminist studies, aesthetic studies, space studies, myth studies, Cather's affinity with contemporary thinkers, pedagogical studies and the like. There was also a scholarly edition of Cather being published, *Willa Cather on Writing: Critical Studies on Writing as an Art,* in 1988. Critical studies on Cather published in the 1990s further solidified her reputation since critics of this decade began to notice that her works, once dismissed as indifferent to real-life concerns, were as a matter of fact, grappled with major themes in American culture and history. Through an examination of five of Cather's novels, Guy Reynolds's *Cather in Context: Progress, Race, Empire* discusses Cather's response to such issues as progressivism, immigration, Americanization, social Darwinism, primitivism and cyclical historiography. In a similar vein, Joseph Urgo argues in *Willa Cather and the Myth of American Migration* that "Cather is a comprehensive resource for the demarcation of an empire of migration in US culture" (1995: 5).

With new findings in the field of biographical studies and gender studies, more theoretical perspectives have been employed to reevaluate Cather's works in the twenty-first century. Cather's fiction has been interpreted in light of various "-isms" and the bulk of this century's scholarship centered on space and place studies and cultural criticism.

As far as Cather's connection with diverse "-ism(s)" is concerned, the majority of critics tend to read Cather's fiction against the literary atmospheres of historical periods. Typical studies of this sort include Susan J. Rosowski's *The Voyage Perilous: Willa Cather's Romanticism*, which deals with Cather's shifting response to "the British brand of Romanticism" represented especially by John Keats, and Jo Ann Middleton's *Willa Cather's Modernism: A Study of Style and Technique*, which tries to find the formative and narrative affinities shared between Cather and the modernists. In 2001, *American Literary Realism* devoted a special issue to Cather's affiliations with the literary school of realism.

Whereas the scholars mentioned above concentrate only on one literary school as it pertains to the formation of Cather's aesthetics, nowadays, it has become common practice for scholars to interpret her writings against a much more complex literary background. Taking Cather's relationship with modernism as an example, more and more scholars have chosen to adopt what Millington calls a "historicist, culture studies" methodology in studying the author's intriguing relationship with modernism.[①] From this perspective, scholars have become less interested in "the formal qualities of Cather's fiction" than in the exploration of "the nature of her engagement with the definitive experiences and ideological movements of twentieth-century life—migration and immigration, nostalgia, progressivism, the emergence of a fully fledged culture of consumption, and so on" (2005: 52). Following this new literary trend, recent years have seen the publication of *Cather Studies* (Vol. 9): *Willa Cather and Modern Cultures*, which is an excellent exploration of Cather's

---

① The debate about Cather's relationship with modernism has been a lively one during the past decade and a good number of academics have been, and are, heavily invested in establishing her modernist credentials. Critics work hard to find Cather's association with modernism in one way or another because they hold the belief that if Cather is categorized as a modernist writer, it will greatly boost her literary reputation. Two of the most ardent advocates for Cather's status as a modernist have been Jo Ann Middleton and Richard Millington.

engagement with what this volume terms "modern cultures". Another book that is worth mentioning is Sarah Cheney Watson and Ann Moseley's *Willa Cather and Aestheticism: From Romanticism to Modernism*. This work represents a landmark in the study of Cather's relationship with certain "-isms", since for the first time, Cather is contextualized against more than one cultural background within one single book.

As one of the most significant American novelists, Willa Cather is often identified as an author of "place". Nebraska is the setting of six of her novels; apart from that, the American Southwest and Quebec City also appear in her fiction. During her lifetime, she not only moved among rural Virginia, frontier Red Cloud, Pittsburgh and New York, but also journeyed around different European countries. Cather's connections with these various places have been analyzed by critics such as Merrill Maguire Skaggs, John N. Swift, Joseph R. Urgo and Janis Stout. Elaborating on the heated discussions of "space, place and cultural geography" over the last thirty-five years (Wegner, 2006: 180), critics are drawn to explore how Cather responds to the "natural, material and social spaces" in her texts (Singley, 2004: 127). Because of this new perspective, ecocritical studies gained prominence in Cather studies in 2002 (Nettels, 2002: 119).

Emerging in the 1990s, "new historicist and cultural criticism" has become a well-established branch in Cather studies. This approach has maintained its momentum till today. In general, the resonance of this "cultural turn" is visible in critics' interest in Cather's attitudes towards popular culture; in her dealings with agents, publishers and magazine editors; and more importantly, in the political and social implications of her literary art (Nettels, 2000: 123). To be specific, scholars like Franz Boas would place Cather in the cultural contexts of her era so as to find the echoes of the new version of anthropology in her fiction and her response to major "cultural debates" of her time. What Eric Aronoff and Richard Millington do in their respective essays, "Anthropologists, Indians, and New Critics: Culture and/as Poetic Form in Regional Modernism" and "Where is Cather's Quebec? Anthropological Modernism in *Shadows on the Rock*", is to connect Cather's project in "Tom Outland's Story" (*The Professor's House*) and *Shadows on the Rock* to the major findings of the anthropologists of her day. By the same token, Christopher Schedler traces in Cather's fiction (from *The Song of the Lark, The Professor's House* to *Death Comes for the Archbishop*) her evolving idea of culture (2002: 85-107). In addition to those above-mentioned works, special mention should be paid to both *Willa Cather and Material Culture: Real-World Writing, Writing in the Real World* and *Willa Cather Newsletter & Review*'s special issue on *Food and Drink and the Art of Willa Cather*.

*Willa Cather and Material Culture* also approaches Cather's life and work from the vantage point of cultural studies. Yet unlike the traditional perspective, this study, the editor argues, attempts to mediate Cather in relation to material objects that appear both in her writings and in her daily life. In her introduction "For Use, for Pleasure, for Status: The Object World of Willa Cather", Stout makes plain the significance of the study of Cather in relation to the material objects: on one hand, "few aspects of Cather show her affinity with modernism so clearly as her attention to and concern with material objects, as these relate to the culture generally"; on the other hand, it is inseparable from other topics that have a long history of scholarly and critical attention, such as her aestheticism (2005: 10-11).

Reading through the whole book, one finds that the articles collected in this collection focus on material culture instead of material objects. Half of these essays deal with the important role material culture of various kinds, such as consumerism, the business practices of the magazine industry and the contemporary discussions of nature education, plays in Cather's creation. Other essays, such as Stout's brief overview of the important role some everyday objects (such as food and clothes) play in both her personal life and writings and Ann Romines' analysis of Cather's attachment to quilts, focus on the analysis of Cather's depiction of material objects, exemplifying the rich meanings that can be extracted from these everyday objects.

Similar to the perspective adopted by critics of *Willa Cather and Material Culture*, the whole issue of *Food and Drink and the Art of Willa Cather* focuses on the examination of one significant constituent of everyday life—food and drink in Cather's works. Food and drink in Cather's fiction is the medium through which scholars trace the author's preoccupation with the social movements of her era. By citing examples from *O Pioneers!*, *The Song of the Lark* and *One of Ours*, Susan Meyer examines

Cather's engagement with the "Pure Food Movement" (qtd. in Romines et al., 2010: 38-47). Having analyzed Cather's representation of food in her works, Andrew Jewell interpreted Cather's engagement with Americanization (2010: 72-76).

These studies and others with similar approaches strike one as exemplary of what is characteristic of cultural studies. A prominent endeavor in cultural studies is to subvert the distinctions in traditional criticism between high literature/art and what are considered as the lower forms. For food, drink and the diverse material objects that appear in our everyday life—these items used to be customarily consigned to neglect and oblivion, they are now considered to have great relevance and broad applicability to the study of literature. Like all the other objects and social practices outside the realm of literature and other arts, these everyday items and practices are now viewed as endowed with meanings that are the products of social forces and conventions—they may either express or oppose the dominant ideology in a culture (Abrams, 2010: 66). Even though some attention has been paid to the analysis of these objects as registering Cather's complex feelings and attitudes towards the major cultural events of her day, with everyday life study emerging as "an important organizing principle and theoretical problem in literary and cultural studies", more theoretical support is needed for such interpretations (Epstein, 2008: 476).

Cather scholarship in China follows tightly the latest developments in America. Cather's short stories and novels were translated into Chinese as early as the 1980s by distinguished scholars like Zi Zhongyun, Dong Hengxun and Zhou Huilin. In 1987, on the occasion of the fortieth anniversary of the death of Cather, a symposium was held in Beijing, reaching a climax in the study of Cather's works. In the 1980s, Cather's name began to appear more and more often in the textbooks of American literary history edited by Chinese scholars. Meanwhile, the number of scholars who show great interest in Cather continues to increase. The horizon of Cather studies is also greatly expanding. So far domestic scholars have touched upon nearly all of the important issues that have been discussed by American scholars. Feminist criticism and gender studies, myth and archetypal criticism and cultural studies are some of the most commonly used methodologies for scholars to approach Cather's works.

Of these topics, place and space studies and cultural criticism are often adopted in the study of Cather's works. These studies are taken in the diverse forms of monographs, book chapters, MA theses, doctoral dissertations and journal articles. Among them, Zhou Ming's dissertation "Toward a Humanistic Spatial Poetics" attempts to explore the "genealogical" spatial consciousness reflected in Cather's different periods of literary production. And other scholars such as Yang Haiyan, Tan Jinghua, Chen Miaoling and Sun Ling interpret Cather's works from the perspective of ecocriticism.

The development of literary studies in China also witnesses the "cultural turn" in Cather studies. A group of scholars read Cather against the social context of her era. Sun Hong's critical essay "The Ghost in the Machine: The Multicultural Complex in Willa Cather's Fiction", Xu Yan's "Tragedies and Achievements of Americanization in *O Pioneers!*" "Whose Ántonia?—*My Ántonia* and Americanization Movement", and Zhou Ming's "Good Citizen's Asylum—National Identification in the Progressive Era Represented in *My Ántonia*" represent this perspective. It is good to see that Cather scholarship in China is advancing in line with the latest trend in Cather studies. Yet compared with the scholarship of Cather in the United States, the research scope of Chinese scholars is obviously not wide enough. In terms of topics involved in place and space studies, few domestic scholars ever discussed Cather's "domestic" spaces or landscapes. Similarly, as far as topics involved in cultural studies are concerned, with the exception of scholar Li Li,[1] there are hardly any systematic elaborations of Cather's aesthetics of everyday life as reflected in such daily activities of living and cooking.

After a literature review of Cather scholarship both at home and abroad, one may ask how we could come up with a theoretical paradigm so as to give a more comprehensive reading of Cather's aesthetics. In her provocative book *Cather and*

---

[1] In the second and the third part of Chapter Six "The Reconstruction of the Past" of her monograph *A Study of Willa Cather's Memory Writing*, Li Li tried to elaborate on the beauty of Cather's everyday life with reference to Lefebvre's famous definition of everyday life in the first volume of his *Critique of Everyday Life*. To make her arguments more convincing, she singled out Cather's kitchens for praise, and her purpose for doing so is to reveal the significance of memory to the reconstruction of one's past.

## Chapter I  The Basics of Willa Cather Novels

*the Politics of Criticism,* Joan Acocella argues that political reading is unquestionably the strongest single trend in Cather criticism since for nearly a century, Cather has been ignored, undervalued, attacked or otherwise marginalized by successive schools of critics, namely, Marxists, New Critics, feminists, multiculturalists and cultural studies critics (2000: 67). In the same book, quoting Susan Rosowski's words, Acocella also expresses her confidence in future Cather studies that would attend the "questions of aesthetics" (Rosowski, 1997: 220). Previous studies do not provide a paradigm to solve the conflicts between a political interpretation and an aesthetic one, yet the interpretations of former scholars could lay a foundation for further elaboration. Acocella's arguments in particular are invigorating, for they prompt me to search for an appropriate approach to analyze Cather's aesthetics without ignoring the political undertone of her texts. The present book attempts to examine Cather's aesthetics from the perspective of everyday life.

Throughout her literary career, Cather attaches great importance to those seemingly mundane aspects of everyday life, which is reflected both in her explanation of how her works come into being and in her critical evaluation of other writers. On *My Ántonia*, she said, "I would dwell very lightly upon those things that a novelist would ordinarily emphasize and make up my story of the little, everyday happenings and occurrences that form the greatest part of everyone's life and happiness" (qtd. in Bohlke, 1986: 44-45). Later, Cather's words in her letter to the editor of *The Commonweal,* explaining how *Death Comes for the Archbishop* came into being,[①] and her letter to Governor Wilbur Cross of Connecticut for his appreciative review of *Shadows on the Rock*,[②] further show how strongly she approves of the literary principle of focusing on the ordinary and the trivial aspects of life in her literary creation.

These are of course not the only occasions on which Cather openly defends

---

[①] Cather said, "in the Golden legend the martyrdoms of the saints are no more dwelt upon than are the trivial incidents of their lives; it is as though all human experiences, measured against one supreme spiritual experience, were of about the same importance."

[②] Cather said, "and really, a new society begins with the salad dressing more than with the destruction of Indian villages."

her selection of materials. In an earlier review on the differences between Mrs. Humphry Ward[①] and George Eliot, Cather argues that George Eliot had what Mrs. Humphry Ward had not, "the red blood of common life", and Cather goes to say that "the author of *Adam Bede* could lay all her own traditions aside and at will confine herself to those simple, elementary emotions and needs that exist beneath the blouse of a laborer" (*KA* 376). On another occasion, she acknowledges her admiration for Katherine Mansfield in this way, "I doubt whether any contemporary writer has made one feel more keenly the many kinds of personal relations which exist in an everyday 'happy family' who are merely going on living their daily lives, with no crises or shocks or bewildering complications to try them" (*KA* 108). In her preface to *The Best Stories of Sarah Orne Jewett*, Cather praises Jewett for having written "the people who grew out of the soil and the life of the country near her heart, not about exceptional individuals at war with their environment" (*WCW* 55). In her affirmative view of these writers' capacities for painting the everyday life of common people, Cather also finds reasons for her choice of writing subjects. To be true, "love affair, courtship, marriage, broken heart or the struggle for success" never seems to be a thematic concern with Cather. The majority of Cather's heroes and heroines, be it Alexandra in *O Pioneers!*, or Ántonia in *My Ántonia*, or Claude in *One of Ours*, are not of noble birth. Instead, Cather chooses to depict the aspects of life that "actually made up the great part of human experience for ordinary people—cooking, eating, working, caring about the friends" (Stout, 2001: 174). Cather's works are well received by readers of different generations for the same reason that they find identification in her depiction of people, settings and situations within their realms of experience, a realm in which they "could feel confident making judgments about the correlation between their world and its artistic depiction" (Johanningsmeier, 2015: 55).

Critics have long noticed Cather's attention to everyday life. In Fryer's opinion, "Cather's landscapes of the imagination begin with the real, the everyday, the

---

① Mary Humphry Ward (1851-1920), a niece of Matthew Arnold, was a British novelist who wrote under her married name as Mrs. Humphry Ward.

experienced" (1986: 249). Millington holds the view that what defines Cather's modernism is her tendency to locate "the field of art in the terrain of the everyday" (2005: 64). Cather's depiction of everyday life experience is highly attractive to critics such as Deborah Carlin, in whose opinion, "only a well-adjusted person could take all of the pain and failure and problems of everyday life and exalt it to the level she does" (1992: 4).

Cather's everyday life depiction ranges from the furnishing of the interior house, to the consumption of food and drink, the clothes and jewelry of her characters, and the application of transportation or communication tools. Even though the majority of scholars do not use the epithet "everyday" to describe what they have noticed as a salient feature in Cather's writing, it is often the case that the words they employ convey meanings similar to that of the "everyday". For example, in his essay published on *The Sewanee Review*, Edward Wagenknecht regards Cather's writing as a fusing of the worlds of Jewett and Whitman, as possessing an aesthetic sense to discipline her love for common things (qtd. in Murphy, 1984: 9). And *The Los Angeles Times* reviewer admires Cather's consistent ability to extract beauty from ordinary things (qtd. in Murphy, 1984: 14). Here both the words "common things and ordinary things" connote something in common with the characteristics of everyday life.

Compared with the sporadic comments on Cather's attention to "everyday, common and ordinary things", there is no lack of studies focusing on Cather's delineation of different aspects of everyday life. Of all the aspects of everyday life, eating draws the greatest attention from scholars. Yet even with this topic, the interest in it is an accumulated one. When Roger L. Welsch and Linda K. Welsch's *Cather's Kitchens: Foodways in Literature and Life* was first published in 1987, the book was a welcome yet unappreciated monograph. But thanks to "the increasing attention being paid to foodways as a subject for serious scholarship and study" (qtd. in Camp, 2002: 111), the book was reprinted by the University of Nebraska Press in paperback in 2002. Slim as the book is, it encompasses a wide range of topics on food that remain the interest of today's scholars. In their monograph, the Welsches not only detail the cook, kitchens and foods appearing in *O Pioneers!*, *My Ántonia*, *One of Ours* and "Neighbor Rosicky", but also point out the importance of food as a literary device in Cather's works: she "used them widely to develop characters, express region, and delineate ethnicity" (Welsch, 1987: xix).

Later scholars further explore in depth topics that have been mentioned in *Cather's Kitchens*. What Shamim Us-Saher Ansari and Lisa Angelella do in their respective doctoral dissertation, "Aesthetic and Environmentalist Organism in Willa Cather's *Death Comes for the Archbishop* and *Shadows on the Rock*" and "Alimentary Modernism" are further examinations of Cather's use of the theme of diet to reveal the regional sensibilities of different ethnical groups. Bearrie Laura Lyn Pogue's dissertation, "Devouring Words: Eating and Feeding in Selected Fiction of Kate Chopin, Edith Wharton, and Willa Cather", shifts critics' attention from eating to feeding in Cather's works, analyzing the role "the traditional feeder, the non-feeder and the nontraditional feeder"[1] plays in Cather's works such as *O Pioneers!* and *My Ántonia*.

In a similar vein, the publication of *Willa Cather's Tables: The Cather Foundation Cookbook*, which is a collection of recipes from her work, her family and friends, the places that are meaningful to her and the Cather Foundation, indicates a boom in studies concerning relations between the food and drink and the art of Willa Cather. The whole issue of *Willa Cather Newsletter & Review: Food and Drink and the Art of Willa Cather* is devoted to the examination of one significant constituent of everyday life—food and drink in Cather's works. Compared with former studies, topics covered in this issue are certainly more diverse. This issue includes studies not only focus on the interpretation of the relationship between food and ethnicity in Cather's fiction, but also touch upon topics such as the correlation between food and public entertainments and social events, and the connection between food and art/taste.

---

[1] In her dissertation "Devouring Words", Pogue classifies the "feeders" in Cather's fiction into "traditional feeders, non-feeders and non-traditional feeders". In her dissertation, Pogue only points out the similarities between women writers at the fin de siècle (Cather included) and nineteenth-century sentimentalist writers. She defines the "non-feeder" as one who is "charged with feeder responsibilities but fails to nourish or sustain and instead affects the downfall of the family". And the "non-traditional feeder" is one who "does not destroy the traditional construct of home and family but re-forms it, a subversion resulting in the survival of the family, not in its destruction".

With respect to interpretation of Cather's delineation of everyday life, what comes next to eating is her attention to the spaces inhabited by characters in her fiction. Like critical attention to eating, Cather's concern with the interior space of home is also well recognized by scholars. Judith Fryer's *Felicitous Space: The Imaginative Structures of Edith Wharton and Willa Cather* explores both the actual and imagined spaces that Cather inhabited, perceived and created. Ann Romines's central concern in *The Home Plot: Women, Writing & Domestic Ritual* is about Cather's repudiation or acceptation of domestic plots throughout her literary career. Caroline Chamberlin Hellman's *Domesticity and Design in American Women's Lives and Literature: Stowe, Alcott, Cather and Wharton* is to examine "the destructive potentials of both domesticity and art by contrasting domestic interiors with the American landscape and examining the forced interstitial spaces of artistic creation" (2011: 7).

These three studies are worth mentioning, for they not only lay out the trajectories and the rich meanings of Cather's domestic plots, but also point out the indispensable role Cather has played in the formulation or subversion of a distinctive literary female domestic tradition. Unlike the former critics' single concentration on the sphere of the domesticity, Diane D. Quantic proposes that two of Cather's novels, *My Ántonia* and *Sapphira and the Slave Girl,* should be read from the perspective of domestic landscape. Diane's concept of domestic landscape blurs the boundaries between private space and public space. Her domestic landscape of the novels includes "the topographical relationship of houses to the surrounding landscape, the physical design of the structures, the relationship of rooms to one another and to the immediate yard outside, and the ways houses reveal the relationships of family members to each other and to the wider community" (2002: 106).

In contrast with the boom in food studies and the comparatively fierce controversy over Cather's delineation of home, Cather's narration of the other facets of everyday life, such as dress and leisure, does not seem to receive enough attention. Yet with the accumulation of new materials on Cather's involvement with the material culture of her age, the other side of Cather is gradually being revealed to the public. For example, letters (exchanged between Cather and her friends) and photographs indicate that clothes play an important role in her life as well. Cather is said to be a woman whose interest in clothes is on one hand directed towards comfort for hiking or working, on the other hand towards the striking effect the clothes may bring about for the transformation of one's persona in public (Stout, 2005: 8-9). Her students at Allegheny High School in Pittsburgh, for instance, were deeply impressed by her "mannish" but "fashionable" style (Hoover, 2002: 43-48). On Cather's costuming of her characters in her fiction, scholars agree that like her authorial and autobiographical masquerades, Cather's costuming of her characters is also a complex element of her work (Elahi, 2009: 171). Yet with a few exceptions, such as Babak Elahi's discussion of the ways how the West is dressed in Cather's characters being one typical example, few scholars seem to attach much importance to the role dresses play in the everyday life of characters.

Of all the important constituent elements of everyday life in Cather's works, less attention is paid to the interpretation of Cather's leisure. Cather may not have had any formal contact with the ideas of Thorstein Veblen proposed in his masterpiece *The Theory of the Leisure Class*, yet many scholars have argued that many of her works, such as *The Professor's House* and "Flavia and her Artists", are fruitful texts for analysis in Veblenian terms. Michael Spindler reads characters from *The Professor's House* (such as Tom Outland and Mother Eve) against Velben's chapter on "the conservation of archaic traits" (2007: 129-132). In her dissertation "Antimodern Strategies", Stephanie Stringer Gross interprets Cather's short story "Flavia and her Artists" against Veblen's notion of conspicuous consumption (2004: 91-144). Like all other theoretical perspectives and methodologies, Veblen's theories and terms help to illuminate Cather's leisure, yet the scope of Veblen's discussion could not encompass all: there are other ways to study Cather's leisure that do not revolve around Veblen.

Cather's fiction is filled with the pulse of oral narrative. The influence of storytelling on Cather's own development as a writer and the important role storytelling plays in her major works has been much explored by recent scholars such as Mildred Bennett, Richard H. Millington, Derek Driedger, Susan Rosowski, Evelyn I. Funda, Lisa Marie Lucenti and Ann Romines. Scholars tend to focus on either the "the acts of storytelling as a distinctive narrative practice" (Millington, 1994: 695) or the function of "the act of storytelling as a dynamic process of negotiation and reciprocity,

Chapter I The Basics of Willa Cather Novels

leading from individualism to involvement, intimacy and ultimately to community" (Funda, 1998: 53). These studies indicate the significance of storytelling both as a stylistic feature and thematic concern to Cather's aesthetics. Yet none of these studies interpret storytelling from that particular perspective of everyday life, nor are there detailed analysis focusing on the exploration of the interactions between storytelling and other forms of everyday activities, such as cooking, quilting and housekeeping.

To sum up, even though there is neither a lack of sporadic comments on Cather's attention to everyday life, nor on one particular aspect of everyday life in her works, more theoretical support is still needed if one wants to understand Cather's delineation of everyday life as an organic whole. Despite these above mentioned aspects of everyday life, further investigation is still possible if they are approached from a more comprehensive and systematic perspective.

This study continues to examine those aspects of everyday life which occupy an important place in Cather's works, yet fail to be explored in previous studies. The study of the aesthetics of everyday life provides an appropriate paradigm for the understanding of Cather's works, for it not only embodies almost all the important concerns of Cather scholars, but also helps to throw light on Cather's thematic concerns and artistic pursuits throughout her literary career. In other words, everyday life serves as a prism through which readers can know how Cather's aesthetics is intertwined with her sense of femininity, place and modernity. In order to give a comparatively sophisticated elaboration on the various dimensions of Cather's everyday life, a theoretical framework on everyday life needs to be set up.

In literature, the origin of everyday narration can be traced back to as far as when the realist novel appeared.[①] Realists' stance on the depiction of the "real" leads to a detailed reportage of the physical minutiae of everyday life—"human beings

---

[①] In *Everyday Life: Theories and Practices from Surrealism to the Present*, Michael Sheringham asserts that historically speaking, the emergence of a concern with everydayness is closely linked to the evolution of styles and genres. Dutch painting of the seventeenth century can be seen globally as a paean to the riches of ordinary experience. Charles Taylor's *The Sources of the Self* is the first book to establish connections between modern selfhood, attitudes to everyday life and the emergence of artistic genres, notably the realist novel.

in their daily lives, attending closely to what we would now call material culture (objects, interior décor, clothes) and to the practices and rituals of daily life—eating, domestic economy, social interaction" (Sheringham, 2006: 41). With the spread of realism, everyday life enters the domain of literature. Yet there are problems lurking behind realism's stress on the "true" or the "real":

> It has become a truism to say that realism, far from offering either a transparent window on reality, innocently relaying a neutral vision, or the "complex vision" of a sovereign author, is a mode of discourse with its own law, conventions, and codes: it is by manipulating these, while at the same time failing to acknowledge their existence, that the realist writer achieves his or her effects.(Sheringham, 2006: 40)

The concept of everyday life did not come forth until the later half of the twentieth century. From 1947 to 1981, the French theorist Henry Lefebvre published three volumes of *Critique of Everyday Life* (which were published respectively in 1947, 1961 and 1981) plus *Everyday Life in the Modern World* to elaborate his idea on everyday life, laying the theoretical foundation for later everyday life studies. Lefebvre's theoretical model and those influenced by it grow out of debates regarding *la vie quotidienne* in mid-century France. In the first volume of *Critique of Everyday Life*, Lefebvre gives his most articulate definition of everyday life:

> Everyday life, in a sense residual, defined by "what is left over" after all distinct, superior, specialized, structured activities have been singled out by analysis, must be defined as a totality… Everyday life is profoundly related to all activities, and encompasses them with all their differences and their conflicts… And it is in everyday life that the sum total of relations which make the human—and every human being—a whole takes its shape and its form… the critique of everyday life studies human nature in its concreteness. (2008: 97)

The works of Henry Lefebvre on everyday life are a fundamental source for Michel de Certeau, as he signals in the introduction to his masterpiece—*The Practice of*

*Everyday Life* (*L'invention du quotidian: Arts de faire*). When de Certeau undertook his research on everyday life in the early 1970s, three out of four of Lefebvre's most significant theoretical works on everyday life had come out, which means "the epistemic legitimacy of 'everyday practices' was well-nigh assured" (Schilling, 2003: 35). Hence, even in the first volume of *The Practice of Everyday Life,* de Certeau is under no obligation to give a concept to everyday life. Instead, he shifts his attention to the demonstration of the "invention" that everyday life reveals. Throughout his whole project, de Certeau seeks to identify the diverse "tactics"[①], such as "camouflage" "tricks", and "ruse" devised by ordinary individuals to operate within yet against a dominant culture (Clark, 1986: 706). And the French title for the first volume of *The Practice of Everyday Life*, *L'invention du quotidian: Arts de faire*, makes it quite clear that, this everyday life of "making do" can be an art, an "art of doing" through which individuals create, produce and invent their lives.

In general, de Certeau's account of the practice of everyday life revolves around a wide range of spheres of daily practices—walking, reading, telling stories and so on. In *The Practice of Everyday Life*[②], whenever storytelling is evoked, more often than not it is intermingled with de Certeau's discussion of the act of narration. Narrative, for de Certeau, covers a wide range of different practices and storytelling is of course only one of the most common practices of de Certeau's "narrative"[③]. The act of narration, or

---

① In Volume One of *Practices*, one of the most influential ideas put forward by de Certeau's is the distinction he made between "strategy and tactics". According to de Certeau, "strategy" is linked to institutions and structures of power, whereas "tactics" are means utilized by individuals to create space for themselves in environments defined by other people's strategies.

② Throughout my book, to distinguish the first from the second volume of *The Practice of Everyday Life*, whenever I mentioned *The Practice of Everyday Life*, it refers to the first volume of the book; the second volume is called *Living and Cooking*.

③ Narrative, for de Certeau, covers a wide range of different practices: from oral traditions of storytelling to the playing and recounting of games; from the micronarratives of proverbs and other forms of popular wisdom to the more elaborated telling of folktales; from condensed advertising narrative to the sprawling and expansive novel. Different as these diverse forms of narrative, one common denominator shared among them is that they are resources that often, if not always, describe and comment on the performance of everyday practice.

telling a story, crops up in several places in *The Practice of Everyday Life*. De Certeau's main points concerning the relationship between storytelling and everyday life can be summarized as follows: stories describe and make comment on the performance of everyday practices. Yet it does not limit itself to that function. As de Certeau consistently emphasizes throughout his project, the significance of storytelling to everyday life lies in what can be made out of the practice of storytelling: it sets models of "tactics, ruses, and coups" that can be employed by storytellers and audiences alike in their everyday life (1984: 19). It is in this sense that narration or the acts of storytelling can be regarded as "an art of saying" or "an art of thinking", which means writers and storytellers alike can employ in their daily life.

Judged by the content of the book, de Certeau does not contribute as much as Luce Giard and Pierre Mayol do. Yet his ideas constitute a framework for Giard and Mayol's collection. In a string of long introductory texts in *Living and Cooking*, Giard acknowledges de Certeau's contribution to the two volumes of *The Practice of Everyday Life* through an elaboration on the genesis of the program. In 1974, a government agency—DGRST (Délégation Générale à la Recherche Scientifique et Technique, which is a general office for science and technology research) asked de Certeau to direct a research program on problems of culture and society.

The two volumes of *The Practice of Everyday Life* are the results of a long-term research project (from the end of 1974 to 1978). To fulfill this mission he was assigned, de Certeau organized three collaborative circles to work on that ambitious and complex program. Luce Giard and Pierre Mayol are the backbone of the "first circle" and the "third circle"[①]. They are also the direct collaborators on the contract

---

① The "first circle" functioned from June 1974 until the spring of 1975. With just a few exceptions, the "first circle" was composed of young researchers in the middle or at the end of their graduate studies. The "second circle" of collaborators involved the doctoral seminar given by de Certeau in anthropology at the University of Paris VII-Jussieu between 1974 and 1978 until his definitive departure for California. The "second circle" basically constituted "the place of experimentation and the echo chamber" where the theoretical propositions of de Certeau were fashioned and tested in diverse contexts. The "third circle" was "a small, restrained, and stable group composed of the direct collaborators on the contract with the DGRST".

with the DGRST. Even though it is Mayol himself who takes full charge of the investigation on the neighborhood and is the sole author of that part in *Living and Cooking*, the proposal to engage in an observational practice in a Paris neighborhood was long given by de Certeau at the very beginning of the program (de Certeau et al., 1998: xxiv). Hence de Certeau's significance to the second volume of *The Practice of Everyday Life* is definitely not limited to the several articles (written by himself) inserted by Giard and Mayol in their book.

When *Habiter, Cuisiner* (*Living and Cooking*) appeared in 1980, it included de Certeau's preface, but not his name. Fourteen years later, when Giard edited and published a revised, expanded edition of the same volume, she and Mayol decided to include de Certeau as a coauthor, for they added several of his articles to their book. More importantly, since de Certeau had "aroused, enriched, and accompanied" their research in so many ways that they "deemed it right and fair, legitimate as well, to salute his memory, to make visible his presence in this volume" (*LC* xlii).

*Living and Cooking* is composed of fourteen texts of varying lengths appertaining to the topic of "le quotidian", based on anthropological fieldwork. The current dissertation benefits from this book in two ways. First, the concept of the neighborhood employed by Mayol is quite useful in the interpretation of Cather's construction of diverse neighborhood in her works. Second, Giard's investigation of women's relationship with the nourishing arts of cooking can be used for reference in the interpretation of the gendered aspect of food and cooking in Cather's works.

Mayol's discussion of the neighborhood revolves around the following two questions: What is the neighborhood? In what sense is the study of the neighborhood pertinent to the study of everyday life? The neighborhood is, in the common sense, for the dweller, "a known area of social space in which, to a greater or lesser degree, he or she knows himself or herself to be recognized" (1998: 9). Or to borrow Mayol's words, the neighborhood appears as "the domain in which the space-time relationship is the most favorable for a dweller who moves from place to place on foot, starting from his or her home. Therefore, it is that piece of city that a limit crosses distinguishing private from public space" (1998: 10).

Different pieces of information can be pieced together from these two definitions. From the former, the neighborhood emerges as the social space in which one's identity is forged. If a dweller wants to be esteemed by those around him or her and to establish an advantageous relationship with those that live in the same neighborhood, he or she has to follow certain "cultural practice"[①]. "A 'practice' is what is decisive for the identity of a dweller or a group insofar as this identity allows him or her to take up a position in the network of social relations inscribed in the environment." (1998: 9) From the latter, the neighborhood is the borderland between the private and public space. The neighborhood consists of not only individual household (the kitchen, the bedroom, the dining room and living room), but also other buildings along the neighborhood streets, grocery stores, churches, the café, and so on. The arrangement of one's interior space—the color or the material of the furniture, for instance, composes a "life narrative", which speaks louder than words about the owner of the house: his or her personal preferences, personality, educational background, family tradition, economic and social status. The grocery stores, cafés, the market, on the other hand, are the meeting place where individuals living in the same neighborhood get together.

The neighborhood is considered as one important spatial parameter for the study of everyday life, for it is the middle term in an existential dialectic (on a personal level) and a social one (on the level of a group of users), between inside and outside (1998: 11). To live in one's neighborhood is thus a process of "a mastery of the social environment". "The reciprocal habituation resulting from being neighbors, the processes of recognition—of identification—that are created thanks to proximity… all these 'practical' elements offer themselves for use as vast fields of exploration

---

[①] According to Pierre Mayol, cultural practice is the more or less coherent and fluid assemblage of elements that are concrete and everyday (a gourmet menu) or ideological (religious or political), at once coming from a tradition (that of a family or social group) and reactualized from day to day across behaviors translating fragments of this cultural device into social visibility, in the same way that the utterance translates fragments of discourse in speech. In Mayol's understanding, cultural practice is always implicitly taken in the anthropological tradition (Morgan, Boas, Frazer, Durkheim, Mauss, Levi-Strauss, etc.). To be specific, it is the underlying value systems structuring the fundamental stakes of everyday life, unperceived consciously by subjects, but decisive for their individual and group identity.

with a view to understanding a little better the great unknown that is everyday life." (1998: 9)

While Mayol's elaboration on the neighborhood provides a perfect geographical angle to the understanding of everyday life as depicted in Cather's fiction, Luce Giard's interpretation of doing-cooking[①] is constructive to the understanding of the gendered aspect of Cather's everyday life. Before the appearance of *Living and Cooking*, there had already been a wave of books theorizing food. Levi-Strauss's elaboration on the raw and the cooked, Mary Douglas's discussions on food taboos, Leo Moulin's study of the pyschosociology of alimentary practices, and Jean-Jacques Hemardinguer's review of a history of alimentation and eating practices exert great impact on the discourse of food. Yet none of them focus on gender. Giard and his colleagues are among the first to pursue specifically the gendered aspects of food production and consumption (Martin, 1999: 209). There are several points that are worth mentioning about Luce Giard's doing-cooking. In the first place, Giard alters the stereotypical views on doing-cooking. Doing-cooking is no longer regarded as a repetitious, basic and humble activity of everyday life. Instead,

> With their high degree of ritualization and their strong affective investment, culinary activities are for many women of all ages a place of happiness, pleasure, and discovery. Such life activities demand as much intelligence, imagination, and memory as those traditionally held as superior, such as music and weaving. In this sense, they rightly make up one of the strong aspects of ordinary culture. (de Certeau et al., 1998: 151)

Yet, Giard has to admit the conflict lying between the culinary activities and those intellectual ones. As a young girl, Giard refused to be an heir to such female tradition because she had always preferred her room, her books and her silent games to the kitchen where her mother busied herself (1998: 152).

---

[①] This expression is a rather awkward translation of the unique phrase that Luce Giard uses to specify the practice of cooking. She uses the inventive term faire-la-cuisine (doing-cooking) to resonate with the underlying theme for both volumes provided by Michel de Certeau in the expression *arts de faire*.

In the second place, through bringing into discussion the question of "what does one eat", Giard establishes strong associations between food and memory and the past. Food is a veritable discourse of the past and a nostalgic narrative about the country, the region, the city, or the village where one was born (1998: 184), which means the food that one eats also becomes a mark, a sign of difference. For instance, the daily diet of a family is a good indicator of the economic situation of the household. Also we can tell easily from the food a family eats whether they are of foreign origins or not. One always holds prejudice against or tends to mistrust the culinary customs of the other. In this sense, the discourse on food is also a "narrative of difference, inscribed in the rupture between the alimentary time of the 'self' and the alimentary time of the other" (Giard, 1998: 184).

In both Mayol's and Giard's sections, a key term that keeps reappearing is propriety. For Mayol, "propriety is the symbolic management of the public facet of each of us as soon as we enter the street" (1998: 17). To put it in another way, propriety is the unwritten rule which exerts great influence on one's ways of how to present oneself to the public: how to dress properly, how to address others properly and so on. Since propriety carries on itself an ethical justification of behaviors that is intuitively measurable, it is important for the dwellers of the neighborhood to be fully aware of its influence and to try one's best to avoid incurring too much chatting and curiosity. According to Mayol, there are two sides to chatting and curiosity (1998:19). On one hand, they are internal impulses absolutely fundamental to the everyday practice of the neighborhood, nourishing the motivation for neighbor relations; yet on the other hand, they constantly try to abolish the strangeness contained by the neighborhood. Chatting in particular functions as "a repeated exorcism against the alteration of the social space of the neighborhood by unpredictable events that might cross it, it seeks 'a reason for everything', and it measures everything against the backdrop of propriety" (1998: 19).

In contrast with Mayol's direct confrontation, propriety as a hidden rule, does not seem to have much to do with Giard's investigation of doing-cooking. But when she does literature review of the cultural significance of the manners of preparing and eating food, she does make reference to Pierre Bourdieu's ideas of table manners as pulled out in his *Distinction: A Social Critique of the Judgement of Taste*. According to Bourdieu, there is great difference between a working-class meal and the bourgeoisie way of eating. Whereas the former group eats mostly out of economic necessity and habit (just a plain eating), the latter eats with all due form (qtd. in de Certeau et al., 1998: 183). Here, to eat and drink with all due form is to behave properly, because eating is always "much more than just eating" (qtd. in de Certeau et al., 1998: 198).

In interpretation of Cather's everyday life, while classification and categorization are convenient and helpful in conceptual terms, the aesthetics of Cather's everyday life is not reducible to the three aspects that are going to be discussed in this study. The practice of the neighborhood, doing-cooking and storytelling constitute three of the most representative aspects of Cather's portrayal of everyday life. Yet in a sense, there is no strict dividing line among de Certeau's discussions of the act of storytelling as an art form and Mayol's and Giard's investigations of the other two distinctive fields of the practice of everyday life—living in the neighborhood and doing-cooking. Hence we need a level of flexibility between chapters in which the act of storytelling often happened when one dined with another and allow for particular concepts, such as propriety to be discussed in different sections. De Certeau's elaboration on the relationship between storytelling and everyday life, Mayol's discussion of the importance of the neighborhood as a spatial parameter for the understanding of the ongoing of everyday life as well as Giard's interpretation of both the gendered and the racial evocation of doing-cooking provide the theoretical framework for my following chapters. A synthesis of these viewpoints helps to verify the complexity of Cather's aesthetics of everyday life.

Theoretical perspectives on everyday life are certainly constructive, yet not sufficient enough for the understanding of Cather's aesthetics of everyday life. To fully grasp Cather's aesthetics of everyday life, we need to take into consideration Cather's particular status as a writer at the turn of the twentieth century, or to put it another way, her relationship with the literary imagination of the fin de siècle. Situated between the Victorian and Modernist periods, the fin de siècle is an exciting and rewarding period to study, for in this decade, "literature was an active and controversial participant within debates over morality, aesthetics, politics and science" (Marshall, 2007). When used in reference to literature, fin de siècle is often employed to describe the movement inaugurated by the decadent poets of France and the movement of aestheticism in England at the turn of the century.

Fred Lewis Pattee, the first "professor of American literature", is one of the few scholars to use this term to describe the American literary scene of that epoch. In his book *The New American Literature, 1890-1930*, Pattee summarizes the literary environment of America during the closing decade of the nineteenth century: there appeared at the very opening of the 1890s a new and vigorous group of young writers, yet the influence of this entire group cannot make a comparison with the revolution brought by Tolstoi and the "realist writers" in Russia; in the north, Ibsen; in France, Flaubert, Maupassant and Zola; in England and Ireland, Aubrey Beardsley, Oscar Wilde and Bernard Shaw. In the words of Pattee, compared with what has happened in the literary world of Europe, America in the nineties furnishes no revolutionists in writing (1937: 14).

Pattee's description offers us the literary milieu during which Cather embarked on her literary career. Even though the majority of Willa Cather's works were composed in the period from the 1910s to the 1930s, her acquisition of artistic training began much earlier. As a student, Cather read widely. By the time she began to write for the *Nebraska State Journal* in the fall of 1893, she had "already studied a good many nineteenth-century classics… with some intensity: the great essayists Carlyle, Ruskin, Pater, Arnold, and Emerson, writers whose beliefs… touched her own" (*KA* 36). Cather's rhetorical shaping of herself in the 1890s and 1900s is strongly framed by these British writers. Cather's later editorial experience in the *Home Monthly Magazine* between the summer of 1896 and 1897 gives her a better chance to get engaged with British writers within the transatlantic salon of publishing and journalism (Reynolds, 2013: 359).

The fin de siècle has a deciding influence on Cather's formation of her everyday life aesthetics. To be sure, the literary milieu of the fin de siècle gave Cather her subject: her sense of who or what might qualify the subject, and the set of attitudes she brings to the treatment of her material. Aestheticism, the New Woman and feminine writing and the question of realism are three of the main currents of radical and innovative thinking at the fin de siècle that are most pertinent to the understanding of Cather's aesthetics of everyday life. Together these three main currents of thinking help not only to shape the particularity of her aesthetics, but also to reveal the intricate relationship among art, gender, politics and everyday life in Cather's writings.

The impact of the fin de siècle on Cather's formulation of artistic principles has long been noticed by scholars. For instance, in his book, *The Landscape and the Looking Glass*, John H. Randall III contends that "Cather grew to literary awareness in the eighteen-nineties; it was the nineties that shaped her artistic consciousness, and she remained a child of the nineties for the rest of her life" (1960: 1). To support his contention, among all the literary and social movements of that era, Randall singles out Art for Art's Sake to elaborate his points. In Randall's opinion, Cather has far more in common with the aesthetes, such as Walter Pater, in their concept of art and of the mission of the artist than with the decadents, such as Oscar Wilde (1960: 6). When Randall tries to explain why he believes Cather has more affinities with Walter than with Wilde, he attributes it to the sharp contrast between Cather's aesthetics and Wilde's. "She was interested in people as people, whereas the decadents on the whole were not… her finest work, the prairie novels and tales, is based on her abiding love for nature" while the decadents "were bored by the nineteenth-century cult of nature worship" and to them "the great glory of art was that it was artifice, and had a design and polish and style which nature lacks" (1960: 5-6).

More and more scholars have taken notice of in Cather's writings the resonance of the late nineteenth century aestheticism represented by Walter Pater and the related Arts and Crafts movement. Sarah Cheney Watson maintains both in her doctoral dissertation "Servant of Beauty: Willa Cather and the Aesthetic Movement" and in her essay "Willa Cather's Disenchanted Epicurean: Godfrey St. Peter in *The Professor's House*" that Cather's understanding of Art for Art's Sake comes from Walter Pater instead of Oscar Wilde. Leona Sevick argues that Cather's criticism of modern values in novels like *O Pioneers!, The Song of the Lark, My Ántonia* and *One of Ours* is the common thread that ties her work to the Art and Crafts movement (Watson and Moseley, 2013: 10). Apart from what has been acknowledged by these scholars, the Art for Art's Sake's influence on Cather would be detected in her school years. In a column of September 23, 1894 from the *Nebraska State Journal* entitled "Commitment", written when she was a senior college student, Cather stated the gospel of Art for Art's Sake movement in her own words:

> In a work of art intrinsic beauty is the raison d'être. Any piece of art is its own excuse for being. Art, like wisdom, is born full-armed without the will or consent of man... No man, or woman, is ever justified in making a book to preach a sermon. It is a degradation of art... An artist should have no moral purpose in mind than just his art... The mind that can follow a "mission" is not an artistic one. An artist can know no other purpose than his art... An artist should not be vexed by human hobbies or human follies; he should be able to lift himself up into the clear firmament of creation where the world is not. (*KA* 406-407)

One may notice the similarities shared between Cather's artistic doctrine and that of the aesthetes: her emphasis on the intrinsic beauty of art, the independence of art from politics or religion (sermon), her insistence that art should become the reason for its own existence (intrinsic beauty is the raison d'être). Not only does Cather clearly state her allegiance to the Art for Art's Sake movement in this column, but many of her other columns reprinted in *The Kingdom of Art* and *The World and the Parish* are punctuated with various names associated with the broader aesthetic movement in France and England. Cather mentions not only Walter Pater and Oscar Wilde but also Théophile Gautier, Charles Baudelaire, Gustave Flaubert, Dante Gabriel Rossetti, Christina Rossetti, Charles Algernon Swinburne, William Morris, Sir Edward Burne-Jones, James A. McNeil Whistler and Henry James (Moseley and Watson, 2013: 7). As in her 1925 introduction to *The Best Stories of Sarah Orne Jewett*, Cather alludes to Pater directly, declaring that just as:

> Pater said that every truly great drama must, in the end, linger in the reader's mind as a sort of ballad... It must leave in the mind of the sensitive reader an intangible residuum of pleasure; a cadence, a quality of voice that is exclusively the writer's own,

individual, unique. A quality that one can remember without the volume at hand, can experience over and over again in the mind but can never absolutely define, as one can experience in memory a melody, or the summer perfume of a garden. (Preface xi)

Here the quality that can be experienced repeatedly but can never absolutely be defined is an echo of her own articulation of "the thing not named"[①] in her essay "The Novel Deméublé"—the inexplicable presence of the thing not named, of the overtone divined by the ear but not heard by it, the verbal mood, the emotional aura of the fact or the thing or the deed, that gives high quality to the novel or the drama, as well as to poetry itself.

Compared with preceding studies that focus on the interpretation of the similarities between Pater and Cather, discussions on the relationship between Cather and Wilde are scant. A scholarly exploration of Cather's response to Wilde's aesthetics helps to foster a fresh understanding of Cather's everyday life aesthetics. Cather's first remark on a performance of Wilde's *Lady Windermere's Fan* (June 4, 1894) is basically a negative one. She modifies a little her judgment of the play when she saw it for the second time (December 17 of the same year), but still she considers it hopelessly artificial. Later, in a review of Robert Hichens' *The Green Carnation* (first published anonymously in November 1894), a satire animated by *The Picture of Dorian Gray*, she deems Wilde's book "inane and Mr. Wilde's epigrammatic school"—aesthetic movement full of "absurd mannerisms" (*WP* 153).

One year later, a week before Wilde's conviction on gross indecency in her article titled "Oscar Wilde: Hélas", Cather calls the aesthetic movement the most fatal and dangerous school of art that has ever voiced itself in the English tongue. She also deems the artistic pursuit of the aesthetic school a complete failure, for what the school has from the beginning set out to seek "has ended by finding what was most grotesque, misshapen and unlovely" (*WP* 154). In this review, Cather also makes a

---

[①] It is interesting to note that this term "the thing not named" is called by O'Brien as a "startling phrase" and a proof of Cather's lesbianism. But from this parallel between Pater's statement and Cather's, maybe "the thing not named" is not that "startling" at all but a commonplace of fin-de-siècle aesthetics.

list of the reasons for her dislike of Wilde's concepts of aestheticism—it is insincere, false, artificial and against human nature. However, these harsh criticisms of Wilde and his school are only part of the whole story. To overstress Cather's dislike of Wilde will lead to a failure to explain why more than once, her short stories hint at Wildean characters and other figures that are related to aesthetic movement: be it the earlier "The Paul's Case" "The Garden Lodge" "The Marriage of Phaedra", or the later "Double Birthday".

In fact, even from the beginning, despite her rebuke of Wilde and aestheticism, Cather is fully aware of Wilde's talents. In the same essay "Oscar Wilde: Hélas", she articulates her harsh criticism of Wilde, lamenting Wilde's tendency to put his wit to false use. "He might have been a poet of no mean order, he might have been one of the greatest living dramatists, yet he commits the sin 'against literature' and 'the holy spirit in man'." (*WP* 264)

Cather appropriates what she finds accordant with her own artistic principles from the doctrine of aestheticism but discards those she believes inconsistent with her own. Hence, she develops an aestheticism of a different type—a type of aestheticism which is deeply rooted into daily life yet above the mundane routine of everyday experience. When Cather criticizes Wilde and his school, it is their being insincere, false and artificial, as well as against human nature that she cannot live with. Therefore, for her own creation, she will stick to the opposites of these qualities. She will follow Sarah Orne Jewett's advice, to find her own "quiet center of life, and write from that to the world that holds offices, and all society, all Bohemia; the city, the country" and in short, she will "write to the human heart, the great consciousness that all humanity goes to make up" (1911: 259).

While aestheticism is famous for being brittle and elitist, reading Cather's work, one senses "the warm current of life" (Wagenknecht, 1994: 222). Characters in Cather's novels and short stories are seldom of noble birth. In her delineation of the common life of common people, Cather challenges the doctrines struck by Wilde and his school. In this way, she puts the term aestheticism to her own use. Cather's aestheticism transcends the exclusiveness of Wilde's aestheticism and becomes instead more comprehensive than what the movement initially advanced. In her opinion, "art thrives best where the personal life is richest, fullest and warmest, from the kitchen up" (*WCP* 149). Also "the farmer's wife who raises a large family and cooks for them and makes their clothes and keeps house and on the side runs a truck garden and a chicken farm and a canning establishment, and thoroughly enjoys doing it all, and doing it well, contributes more to art than all the culture clubs" (*WCP* 47). Therefore, both Ántonia in *My Ántonia* and Cécile in *Shadows on the Rock* fall into artists of high rank. Cather's statement of the "a esthetic appreciation begins with the enjoyment of the morning bath" reminds us readers of Thea's (the heroine of *The Song of the Lark*) epiphany when she takes a bath in the great Canyon.

If interpretation of the other side of Cather's relationship with Wilde helps to deepen our understanding of the aesthetic aspect of Cather's depiction of everyday life, nuanced reading of her portrayal of new women characters gives hints as to the gendered aspect of her everyday life aesthetics. Cather received her literary training in an age when the New Woman became not only a social fact but also a constant presence in the writings of male and female writers alike. As an embodiment of new values, the New Woman poses a critical challenge to the existing social order and exerts great influence on the American national literature. From the 1890s, "the New Woman—independent, outspoken, iconoclastic—empower the work of Kate Chopin, Alice James, Charlotte Perkins Gilman, Edith Wharton, Ellen Glasgow, Willa Cather, and the young Gertrude Stein" (Elliot, 1988: 589). New Woman fiction, such as Sarah Orne Jewett's *A Country Doctor* and Kate Chopin's *The Awakening* challenge the received wisdom on courtship, marriage and the family, rejecting such truths as the maternal instinct and the role of child-rearing as the highest duty of women.

Like her seniors, Cather is much provoked by the figure of the New Woman. Cather's fascination with the New Woman figure can be detected as early as the end of the nineteenth century. On November 16, 1895, in a column on the current literary scene for the *Lincoln Courtier*, Willa Cather praises Henry James as "that mighty master of language and keen student of human actions", but wishes he would write "about modern society, about 'degeneracy' and the New Woman and all the rest of it" (qtd. in Curtin, 1970: 275). Apart from these direct comments, Cather's "mannish attire, short hair", her "high, stiff collars, string or four-in-hand ties and mannish white cuffs", her marital status as a single woman throughout her life, her determination to attend college and pursue a professional career, and her preoccupation with characterization of numerous educated or economically independent women all seem to testify to the validity of the assumption of Cather as a "New Woman" (Woodress, 1987: 69-70).

Yet Cather "evades classification and unsettles facile, reductive interpretations" (Rosowski, 2011: 250). Cather's affirmative reviews of new women figures during the 1890s align her with some of the core values represented by New Woman.① But when it comes to the New Woman fiction of the same period, Cather holds an unfavorable opinion on their writing subjects and thematic concerns. She lambastes Sarah Grand's widely popular feminist novel *The Heavenly Twins* as "atrocious" and decries its "cheap, vulgar, ignorant discussions of questions that should not be touched outside of a medical clinic" (*WP* 132). For Chopin's *The Awakening*, she asks why, given Chopin's "exquisite and sensitive, well-governed… style", she devoted her narrative to "so trite and sordid a theme" (*WP* 697).

The disparity between Cather's fascination with new women figures and her criticism on New Woman fiction shows the complexity of Cather's "New Woman Complex". Critic Janis P. Stout calls Cather a resistant New Woman, for he considers her a New Woman who commits to "notions of personal singularity who refused to fit any prepared mold" (2000: 123). Similarly, Alexandra in *O Pioneers!* is named by Reginald Dyck as a reluctant New Woman pioneer for "circumstances force her to take a role that would normally have gone to one of the brothers" (2013: 171). Pearl James makes a distinction between the fact of Cather as a New Woman, who "challenged professional and literary notions of women's proper sphere" (2013: 92) and her characterization of the New Woman as a dangerous and threatening figure

---

① Around the year of 1896, in a biographical sketch on the wives of presidential candidates William McKinley and William Jennings Bryan for the socially conservative *Home Monthly*, Cather lauded both wives as new women. While the former demonstrates her capability of doing her work "better and more thoroughly than any man", the latter is "the New Woman type at its best". Mrs. Bryan is an avid reader, an attorney admitted to the bar in Nebraska, clubwoman, wheelwoman, and expert swimmer, also she is quite devoted to her husband's political career and her children.

(Enid in *One of Ours* as a case in point).

Critical studies such as these above mentioned take note of the complexities of Cather's "New Woman Complex", yet more often than not, they fail to specify the very reasons for the seeming contradictions in Cather's narration of the New Woman. Nor have they given nuanced reading of Cather's different types of new women in her fiction. Sandra M. Gilbert and Susan Gubar once commented that "Cather's distrust of the new women was matched by her ambivalence toward her female literary inheritance" (*WP* 175). Their arguments lead me to reflect upon Cather's new women figures against the background of female domestic literary tradition.

In turning her attention to new women figures who either devote themselves to the pioneering of new territory or to the development of her career, Cather seems to subvert the traditional domestic plot which is one of the major concerns to Harriet Beecher Stowe and Sarah Orne Jewett. Yet judged by her preoccupation with the detailed depiction of everyday activities, such as housekeeping, cooking and so on, one can infer that she is not that far away from her female literary forebears. More often than not, domesticity still serves as an important background against which these new women figures can be measured. It is the new women figures who handle well both domestic duties and their professional life that seem to win the favor of the author. New women figures that hanker for missions but neglect their duty to their family are judged harshly by the author.

Much like her reaction to aestheticism, the New Woman and the feminine writing, Cather's affiliations with realism is also very intriguing. Cather grows up and receives her education in a literary world thoroughly permeated by the presence of realism. At first glance, Cather's stress on the depiction of everyday life is quite in line with that advocated by realists represented by William Dean Howells. Yet Cather is not a mere realist of everyday life. Loretta Wasserman observes that, by date of birth, Cather could fit with the precursors of modernism, yet her narrative style, only gently experimental, and her settings—the monotonous plains—consigned her at first to the "realists of the everyday" (1991: 9). In Wasserman's context, the realists of everyday life is a slightly pejorative term. With this label, Cather is relegated to an author with no sophistication and her texts deemed not as innovative as those of the modernists'. We can juxtapose Wasserman's remarks on Cather with the Left Critics' accusation of Cather's aesthetics. If the major discrepancy between Cather and Trilling and Hick lies in their different attitudes toward what should be represented in fiction, the major gap between Cather and the realists rests with the manner in which the subject might be represented in fiction. Along with the general recognition of Cather's canonical status, these arguments against Cather have been proved invalid.

For Cather's involvement with realism, much has been explored. To take *American Literary Realism*'s special issue on Willa Cather as an example, three aspects have been attended by Cather scholars on this topic: first, how Cather selects and simplifies her material against realists' too crowded description (Stout); second, how she negotiates the relationship between realism and romance (Seivert; Murphy); last, how she buries her social criticism under tranquil daily life, avoiding realism's preaching about the social function of literature (Petrie). A comprehensive review of scholarship on the analysis of Cather's affiliations with realism helps to clarify the controversy centering on Cather's depiction of everyday life. Why does Cather choose to depict everyday life in her works? What makes her depiction of everyday life different from those by the realists? Did Cather really fall into supine romanticism in her later works? If not, how could she deal with the "cruelty and rapacity that are so integral a part of it" (Hicks, 1967: 147), in her later works without making sacrifice for her aesthetic ideals? Independent as these questions may look at first glance, they are quite inseparable from one another. Together they reveal the various forces that are at work in Cather's narration of everyday life.

Throughout this book, after providing the literary background against which Cather formulates her everyday life aesthetics, I structure my chapters according to the various dimensions that Cather invokes in her fiction. The practice of the neighborhood, doing-cooking and storytelling are three of the most important parameters to evaluate the significant role that everyday life plays in Cather's fiction. By analyzing each of these three parameters, I will take into account the aesthetic, the gendered and the political aspects of such practice of everyday life.

# Chapter II
# The Practice of the Neighborhood

It is not difficult to discern the main thrusts of the second volume of *The Practice of Everyday Life*, which locates everyday life in the very sphere of the neighborhood. The neighborhood serves as an appropriate parameter for the study of everyday life because according to Pierre Mayol, "the neighborhood is the middle term in an existential dialectic (on a personal level) and a social one (on the level of a group of users), between inside and outside". (qtd. in de Certeau et al.,1998: 11) To live in one's neighborhood is therefore a process of "a mastery of the social environment" and more than that, "the reciprocal habituation resulting from being neighbors, the processes of recognition—of identification—that are created thanks to proximity... all these 'practical' elements offer themselves for use as vast fields of exploration with a view to understanding a little better the great unknown that is everyday life". (qtd. in de Certeau et al., 1998: 9)

Even though it is a common practice to view the neighborhood as one of the significant spatial parameters of everyday life, the neighborhood has not been given much attention until now, as it has long been relegated to the domestic, or even the private sphere. Scholars and non-scholars alike have not given the domestic sphere as much attention as they have given to the public sphere. So Mayol's definition of the neighborhood, his descriptions of the goings on of everyday life in the neighborhood have garnered attention, particularly since scholars have held so few expectations for everyday and domestic life, giving much more attention to the goings on in the public domain. Long held has been the opinion that "Real" events happen somewhere else—on the regional, national or international stages that are beyond the range of everyday life (Sheringham, 2006: 24).

In his preface to *The Practice of Everyday Life*, de Certeau informs us that to *habiter* is to enjoy the "fine art of dwelling" (1984: ix-x). In Mayol's context, since the particular locale he chooses for the study of everyday life is the neighborhood, to know well the fine art of dwelling is to grasp the concept of the practice of the neighborhood, as well as to understand Mayol's definition of that practice:

> The practice of the neighborhood is a tactic collective convention, unwritten, but legible to all dwellers through the codes of language and behavior; any submission to these codes, just as any transgression, is immediately the object of commentary: a norm exists and it is even weighty enough to play the game of social exclusion when faced with "eccentrics", those who "are not or do not act like us". (qtd. in de Certeau et al., 1998: 16)

The impact of the practice of the neighborhood is powerful, to be sure. In order to cope with the constraint set by this unwritten convention, Mayol brings the concept of propriety into discussion.

> Propriety is the symbolic management of the public facet of each of us as soon as we enter the street. Propriety is simultaneously the manner in which one is perceived and the means constraining one to remain submitted to it; fundamentally, it requires the avoidance of all dissonance in the game of behaviors and all qualitative disruption in the perception of the social environment. (qtd. in de Certeau et al., 1998: 17)

Yet to remain submitted to the doctrine of propriety and to avoid all dissonance in the game of the behaviors and all qualitative disruption unfold only part of the story as to the way how propriety works. At the level of behaviors, propriety is a compromise reached between the individual and the neighborhood. By renouncing individual impulses, the individual shows his or her respect to that social contract and in this way "makes a down payment to the collectivity" (qtd. in de Certeau et al., 1998: 8). Yet he or she does not make his or her sacrifice with no purpose. There is some compensation for this coercion for the dweller, such as his or her certitude will be recognized, and he or she will be well thought of by those around her, and thus "founding an advantageous relationship of forces in the diverse trajectories that he or she covers" (qtd. in de Certeau et al., 1998: 9). Mayol's definition of the neighborhood as well as his discussion of tactics involved in the practice of the neighborhood offers a perspective for the discussion of the neighborhood in Cather's major works.

Willa Cather is a good delineator of both domesticity and neighborhood, especially considering that six of her fictional villages are based on her childhood hometown Red Cloud, Nebraska. Red Cloud is the Black Hawk of *My Ántonia*, the Hanover of *O Pioneers!*, the Moonstone of *The Song of the Lark*, the Sweet Water of *A Lost Lady*, the Frankfort of *One of Ours*, and the Haverford of *Lucy Gayheart*. For the strong imprint it bears on her writings, the town itself has become synonymous with Cather's name.

Ann Romines, Caroline Chamberlin Hellman and Judith Fryer are representative scholars who turn their attention to Cather's narration of domesticity. Compared with attention to Cather's delineation of home plot, even though the neighborhood occupies an important place in her works, with a few exceptions, such as Helen Fiddyment Levy's brief mention of the importance of the individual woman's discovery of her membership in the female community (female community functions as a kind of neighborhood) as the source of her creativity in Cather's works, seldom are there studies on this topic (1992: 12),① let alone the study of the neighborhood

---

① One should not deny the fact that there is indeed a direct correlation between the study of neighborhood and the study of community: both can be used to refer to a particular area inhabited by a group of people who share common values. For instance, Quebec in Cather's *Shadows on the Rocks* can be called both as "the neighborhood of Quebec" and "the community of Quebec". But great differences do exist between the connotations of these two words. One of the differences is that unlike neighborhood, communities are not necessarily limited within nearly geographical areas. For instance, in the case of Levy's study of the female community in Cather's works, Thea's epiphany has much to do with her discovery of her membership in the female community which dates back to ancient times.

as a significant constituent of everyday life. The study of the neighborhood in Cather's works is of great significance, since the neighborhood not only serves as the background against which the main plots are developed, but also functions as a vast field of exploration with a view to understand the reciprocal relationship among different community members.

This chapter focuses on the interpretation of the spatial parameters of Cather's everyday life in the neighborhood as reflected in her major works. In the analysis of the neighborhood appearing in Cather's fictions, three aspects are noteworthy. First, the arrangement of one's interior space in one particular neighborhood in Cather's works often reflects the social contexts that are central motifs in her fiction. The domestic life in *Sapphira and the Slave Girl* embodies not only the Colberts' social status, but also the power relationships at work, relationships such as that between the husband and the wife, and the one between the Colberts' and their neighbors. Second, the dwellings in the neighborhood of *Shadows on the Rock* and *A Lost Lady*, arranged in a specific landscape, unveil much about the hierarchical structures of the community, hence indicating the relationships among different social classes, ethical and religious groups. Finally, both the spatial arrangement of the dwellings and the objects found in the adjacent environment exert great impact on individuals who live or tour around the place. While Thea Kronborg's experiencing of the everyday life of those bygone residents of Panther Canyon in *The Song of the Lark* changes the course of her life, Tom Outland's exploration of the daily life of Cliff City in *The Professor's House* extends his definition of civilization, history, and his own place in it.

## 2.1 The Political Side of Domesticity in *Sapphira and the Slave Girl*

*Sapphira and the Slave Girl* is Cather's last novel, yet it is her first major fiction that is set in her birthplace, the Shenandoah Valley of northern Virginia. *Sapphira and the Slave Girl* is about the story of Sapphira Dodderidge Colbert, a privileged white woman. The setting of the story is Back Creek of Virginia in the year of 1856. Sapphira was in her middle-age, crippled by dropsy yet capable enough to manage quite well her household. The domestic atmosphere was peaceful if not harmonious until Sapphira overheard a quarrel between two of her slaves. She began to develop

## Chapter II  The Practice of the Neighborhood

a paranoid fear that her husband Henry, whom she married beneath her status, might have an affair with the slave girl named Nancy, who was a beautiful mulatto. Giving way to her suspicion, Sapphira invited her impudent nephew Martin to destroy Nancy. Nancy felt helpless and went to seek help from Sapphira's daughter Rachel. With the help of Rachel and her abolitionist neighbors, Nancy fled to Canada. For what she had done for Nancy, Rachel was requested by her mother to make no further visits at her house. The mother and the daughter kept their distance from each other until one of Rachel's little girls died of illness and hence brought about reconciliation. The story in the epilogue happened twenty five years later when Nancy returned to Back Creek in silken robes. By the end of the story, Cather unveiled herself to be a five-year-old child who witnessed Nancy's glorious return and heard the stories of those involved in *Sapphira and the Slave Girl.*

Critics in the past tended to read *Sapphira and the Slave Girl* as a minor work because, in some respects, it does not meet their expectations for Cather's novel. *My Ántonia* constitutes the center of her oeuvre, followed by *O Pioneers!*, *The Professor's House* and *Death Comes for the Archbishop* and the like. *Sapphira and the Slave Girl* remained largely marginalized until Toni Morrison addresses the source of its flaws and the conceptual problems that the book both poses and represents in her famous book of literary criticism, *Playing in the Dark: Whiteness and the Literary Imagination*, which draws critics' attention to this much neglected work. The rich meaning of *Sapphira and the Slave Girl* is explored to the utmost thanks to the research into Cather's southern heritage, which culminated in *Willa Cather's Southern Connections: New Essays on Cather and the South*. More than half of the essays in this collection center on *Sapphira and the Slave Girl*. While critics such as Tomas Pollard defend Cather's strategy of containment, other critics such as Marilyn Mobley McKenzie assert that by leaving "unspeakable matters unspoken", Cather perpetuates "the attendant racial ideologies that sustain them" (2000: 87-88).

Apart from attention given to Cather's treatment of race and slavery, critics such as Judith Fetterley and Joseph R. Urgo warn readers against drawing easy conclusions in reading Cather and hence turn readers' attention to "the other side"[①] of Cather's works. In "Willa Cather and 'the old story': *Sapphira and the Slave Girl*", Ann Romines advances Fetterley's and Urgo's contention, pointing to "the persistent, intimate presence of the Terrible" that lies under the pleasant surfaces of *Sapphira and the Slave Girl* (2005: 211). As if such arguments were not convincing enough to attest to the excellence of Cather's last novel, in the historical essay and explanatory notes to the scholarly edition of *Sapphira and the Slave Girl*, Romines goes a step further to call the novel Cather's "most politically confrontational book" (2009: 297-299).

Such contemporary evaluations suggest infinite possibilities in reading Cather's text. The new interest in *Sapphira and the Slave Girl* also indicates that previous scholars seemed to believe that the excellence of the novel can be appreciated only along political lines. To unfold the political side of Cather's text helps to put right the accusation of Cather as an escapist and to inform readers of the fact that Cather is as a matter of fact fully aware of the social reality of her era. Nevertheless, Cather's texts do not have to be politically good. In Cather's view, economics and art are strangers, and art should not be devoted to propaganda for economic or social reform (*WCW* 27). In the light of her remarks, it is not groundless to infer that Cather would dislike the idea of reading her text too politically.

Even though *Sapphira and the Slave Girl* is set in slave-holding Virginia, Cather's focus in her last novel is not on slavery itself. She disapproves of Stowe's *Uncle Tom's Cabin* simply for the reason that she considers it the embodiment of the feminine mind "hankering for hobbies and missions" (*KA* 406). What Cather attempts to do in *Sapphira and the Slave Girl* is the same as what she has kept doing in her former novels. Explicating the process of how *My Ántonia* comes into being, Cather says, "There was the material in that book for a lurid melodrama. But I

---

[①] According to Christopher Benfey, the study of the other side to Cather's fiction has governed much of the criticism in the past ten or fifteen years. The other side Benfey refers to mainly includes the following three aspects: the study of the abundance of "tropes of doubleness and duplicity" in Cather's works; the study of "the concealed key to Cather's narrative lock"; and "the fissure in Cather's career, a perceived break" between her early works and late ones.

## Chapter II The Practice of the Neighborhood

decided that in writing it I would dwell very lightly upon those things that a novelist would ordinarily emphasize and make up my story of the little, everyday happenings and occurrences that form the greatest part of everyone's life and happiness." (qtd. in Bohlke, 1986: 44-45) For *Death Comes for the Archbishop*, Cather confesses that what she "felt curious about was the daily life of such a man [Archbishop Lamy] in a crude frontier society" (*WCW* 7). In defense of her choice of the subject matter in *Shadows on the Rock*, she says she has more interest in the ongoing of "an orderly little French household" than in "Indian raids or the wild life in the forests" (*WCW* 16). Judging from these statements, what fascinates Cather in *Sapphira and the Slave Girl* is still the everyday life of the Colberts and those around them in the same neighborhood. Or, to put it another way, what captures the author's imagination is the impact of economic as well as political forces, i.e., slavery, on the daily routine of the Colberts and their neighbors.

To explore the correlation between the everyday life of the Colberts and their neighbors and the workings of economic and political factors, one can easily turn to Pierre Mayol, whose elaboration on the the neighborhood is particularly insightful. According to Mayol, the neighborhood serves as an appropriate parameter for the study of everyday life because geographically it builds a bridge between interior space and public space. More importantly, it works as a prism through which the often hidden interpersonal relationships among different members of the neighborhood could be reflected off the surface (qtd. in de Certeau et al., 1998: 11-19). In the case of *Sapphira and the Slave Girl*, through Cather's description of the daily routine of the Colberts, readers can glimpse their domesticity. Furthermore, they get to know the intricate relationships between the husband and the wife, the mother and the daughter, the master and the servants, the mistress and the servants, and the servants among themselves. Out of the domestic life of the Colberts, readers can also discern the information about how the Colberts are regarded by their neighbors and vice versa.

As far as the title of the opening chapter of *Sapphira and the Slave Girl*—"The Breakfast Table" suggests, what readers can tell what Cather tries to delineate in this part should have been the most domestic scene in her works. Yet under the surface of a seemingly harmonious dining atmosphere, something odd lurks in every corner of the breakfast table. Cather informs her readers of the hard fact that breakfast is the only meal Henry Colbert shares with his wife, coming straight to breakfast from his workplace [the mill] rather than their shared bedroom. More curiously, his wife seems to be indifferent to his presence at the dinner table, so much so that "she never questions as to his whereabouts" (*SSG* 3). With the exception of the husband's rather formal salutation to his wife, there is no cordial conversation going on at the table. The presence of the colored servant as well as the mention of the kitchen utensils—"a silver coffee urn which stood on four curved legs" may indicate wealth and social status, yet they could not help to alleviate the sense of awkwardness and alienation between the husband and the wife. After a brief introduction of the breakfast scene, the narrator breaks in to notify readers of the opinions the neighborhood has of the Colberts:

> Neither the miller nor his wife was native here: they had come from a much richer county, east of the Blue Ridge. They were a strange couple to be found on Back Creek.
>
> The people of Back Creek and Timber Ridge and Hayfield never forgot that he (Henry) was not one of themselves… His grandfather had come over from Flanders. Henry was born in Loudoun County and had grown up in a neighborhood of English setters. He spoke the language as they did, spoke it clearly and decidedly. This was not, on Back Creek, a friendly way of talking.
>
> His wife also spoke differently from the Back Creek people; but they admitted that a woman and an heiress had a right to. (*SSG* 3-5)

Viewpoints such as these reveal not only the possible reasons for the alienation between the husband and the wife, but also the hierarchical value system that is at work in the community.

Henry Colbert is noted for his fair dealing and regarded as a trustworthy miller in the neighborhood. Yet he is scarcely liked. To the people of Back Creek and Timber Ridge and Hayfield, Henry is always a stranger, which has much to do with not only his foreign origin, but also his own symbolic management of the public

## Chapter II  The Practice of the Neighborhood

facet of himself in the neighborhood (qtd. in de Certeau et al., 1998: 17). Henry is silent and uncommunicative and this is a trait his neighbors do not like. Moreover, he speaks the language clearly and decidedly, with no trace of a southern accent—a style of speaking the neighbors regard as offensive (*SSG* 5). Economically, Back Creek, the neighborhood the Colberts presently live in, is less cultivated than Loudoun County, the neighborhood they move away from. Due to Henry's foreign origin, people in Back Creek feel reluctant to grant him that kind of superiority they are compelled to give his wife for they admitted that a woman and an heiress had a right to speak differently, but a miller is certainly not entitled to speak in such an arrogant way (*SSG* 5). To some degree, the speech prejudice the locals of Back Creek hold against Henry is derived from the distinction that the townspeople make between Henry and themselves. In showing the different attitude the town people hold towards Henry and Sapphira, Cather unmasks the social and racial relationships of that community.

Different from Henry's bluntness in his management of the public facet of himself, Sapphira is keenly aware of the emblematic meanings of different manners of speaking. Sapphira always speaks properly and correctly on various occasions—she is aware of how to vary her tone when addressing people of different status and of different relations to her (Zhu, 1998: 72). To her husband, whom she marries below her status, Sapphira talks in her bland and considerate voice to him when she tries to win him on her side (*SSG* 7). Yet she is also capable of letting her voice become icy or mockingly bitter when he acts against her will. To her servants, based on her personal preference, Sapphira is capable of showing both great kindness and sometimes, cold cruelty (*SSG* 169). Mrs. Colbert's greetings to Mrs. Bywaters, the postmistress of the neighborhood, are marked with civility because she takes a different stand from Mrs. Bywaters on the subject of slavery (*SSG* 37).

Sapphira's sense of propriety is reflected not only in the manner in which she speaks to others, but also in the way she responds to others' imprudence. Sapphira scolds the old coachman Jeff severely for driving out with no shoes on (*SSG* 33). Meanwhile she warns another servant Lizzie not to put disgrace on her on the occasion of Jezebel's funeral, in case the neighbors would gossip about her stinginess (*SSG* 99). Seeing the way her husband talks to the young slave Nancy at the funeral, Sapphira is irritated by the impropriety her husband has shown in public. "Whatever he was pressing upon that girl, he was not speaking as master to slave; there was nothing to suggest that special sort of kindliness permissible under such circumstances... He had forgotten himself." (*SSG* 103-104) Furious as Sapphira is, she is able to restrain herself—"Sapphira had put her handkerchief to her eyes, afraid that her face might show her indignation" (*SSG* 103).

Sapphira's sense of propriety has much to do with her sense of superiority. Sapphira's mother came from England and Sapphira herself was raised in the prosperous Chestnut Hill. Sapphira's mind is thus very hierarchical. Despite her display of superficial politeness towards her neighbors, Sapphira never considers them her equal. In her eyes, inhabitants in Back Creek are "common people" at best and "mountain trash" most of the time (*SSG* 16-33).

In *Sapphira and the Slave Girl*, next to Sapphira, another character who takes place and proper speech most seriously is Till, Nancy's mother. In Till's case, the meaning of place can be defined in two ways. First of all, place can refer to the actual location of different household in the neighborhood. In *Sapphira and the Slave Girl*, it is from Till's perspective that readers have access to the layout of the hierarchical structure of the neighborhood. "People of some account" live in Romney; "the poor white trash" live in the cabins on the slopes of the North Mountain; the "well-to-do" families live along the big road that leads to Winchester; and the "quality" lived in houses surrounded by shaded trees and lawns (*SSG* 73-74). Secondly, one's sense of place can also be used to refer to one's position within the rigid social hierarchy.

Before she was bought by Mrs. Colbert, Till received strict training in social manners from Mrs. Matchem—the housekeeper of Chestnut Hill. Even when she was a little girl, Mrs. Matchem impressed upon Till the big difference "between doing things exactly right and doing them somehow-or-other" (*SSG* 71). For both Mrs. Matchem and Till, propriety carries on itself an ethical justification of behaviors that is intuitively measurable (qtd. in de Certeau et al., 1998: 17). Till never "dawdles over her work" for according to the lessons she has received from Mrs. Matchem, "the shuffling foot is the mark of an inferior race" (*SSG* 40). Since Mrs. Matchem has taught her to value position, to be respectable and well-place becomes the number

## Chapter II The Practice of the Neighborhood

one desire of Till's life (*SSG* 72). Till always wears "a black dress and white apron, neat shoes and stockings" (*SSG* 72). She is very proud of her carriage and deportment and speech. She knows "how to stand when receiving orders, how to meet visitors at the front door, how to make them comfortable in the parlor and see to their wants" (*SSG* 31). Till's possession of the manners of propriety helps her win favor from Sapphira. She is exempted from all the heavy work of a big country house. At first glance, it seems that the comparatively "conspicuous leisure and attire" Till enjoys contributes to her own reputation, yet it is her master and mistress who gain the most from that "vicarious consumption" (Veblen, 2007: 120-121).

In studies after Morrison's 1992 reading of *Sapphira and the Slave Girl*, many readers argue that Cather's characterization of the African Americans in *Sapphira and the Slave Girl* is not as reliable as her characterization of the whites (Romines, 2005: 209). For her dedication to her mistress, Till is often considered as a flat character. But I contend that Till is not a character without depth. Cather does a lot of foreshadowing in the previous chapters to help to explain Till's hierarchical mindset and her acquiescence in her fate. Cather devotes the second chapter of Book Two of *Sapphira and the Slave Girl* to the narration of Till's childhood experiences: how she watched helplessly as her mother burned to death, how she was "literally" adopted by the housekeeper at Chestnut Hill, and how she was trained to be a professional housekeeper. These early experiences are significant for they help to explain Till's acceptance of her mistress's arrangement of her marriage and her muteness with regard to her own daughter's abuse and disappearance.

Till speculates hundreds of times on the reasons why Nancy has fallen out of favor with her mistress. But she never questions anyone of the possible reasons. Like Old Washington, she understands perfectly that "tattling was sure to get a house-man into trouble" (*SSG* 59). When Till is informed of her daughter's disappearance and her possible death, Till seems apathetic. Bluebell, another slave of the Colberts', thinks that it seems that Till does not miss her girl very much (*SSG* 244). Till's appearance of indifference to Nancy's suffering and her display of apathy on the matter of her only daughter's disappearance are what have caused Morrison to complain about the lack of coherence in Cather's handling of the mother-daughter relationship in

*Sapphira and the Slave Girl*. Not until the disturbance caused by Nancy's flight is almost over does Cather insert a furtive exchange between Till and Rachel:

> Till asked in a low, cautious murmur, "You ain't heard nothin', Miss Rachel?"
>
> "Not yet. When I do hear, I'll let you know. I saw her in good hands, Till. I don't doubt she's in Canada by this time, amongst English people."
>
> "Thank you, mam, Miss Rachel. I can't say no more. I don't want them niggers to see me cryin'. If she's up there with the English folks, she'll have some chance." (*SSG* 249)

In Morrison's view, the above passage seems to "come out of nowhere because there had been nothing in a hundred or so pages to prepare us for such maternal concern" (1992: 22). Till's abrupt change of attitude towards her daughter may leave readers unprepared and bewildered. From the perspective of Morrison, the cause of such fragmentation has much to do with Cather's exclusion of the "historical discourse on slave parent-child relationships and pain" (1992: 22). Morrison's elaboration is well-founded as far as the thesis statement of her book is concerned. Yet Cather's insertion of the exchange between Till and Rachel is not as abrupt as Morrison has thought.

The moment Till finds out her daughter's loss of favor, she has tried to impart her own experience to her daughter to remedy the situation:

> "An' if I was you, I wouldn't carry a tray to Missus with no haing-dawg look. I'd smile, an' look happy to serve her, an' she'll smile back."
>
> "…if you smile right, an' don't go shiverin' like a drowned kitten. In all Loudoun County Miss Sapphy was known for her good mannahs, an' that she knowed how to treat all folks in their degree." (*SSG* 44-45)

This episode indicates that Till is not as cold-hearted as she is accused of being. She shuts her eyes to what was going on over at the miller's house not because she does not care about the welfare of her only child, but because of the fact that, with the exception of the knowledge she has inherited from her mentor, Mrs. Matchem,

Till has no other survival tactics she could possibly hand down to her daughter, even when her daughter is being abused. When the only possible solution she has possessed proves to be ineffective, Till has no other option but to side with her mistress. By keeping silent on the arrangement of her own as well as her daughter's fate, Till actually follows the same path as Mrs. Matchem took when Till was sold to Mrs. Colbert. Despite her dissatisfaction with her mistress's selling of her favorite disciple, Mrs. Matchem did not complain, she only "looked down her long nose and compressed her lips" (*SSG* 72). After all, in the words of Rachel,

> Till had been a Dodderidge before ever she was Nancy's mother. In Till's mind, her first duty was to her mistress. Ever since Mrs. Colbert had become an invalid, Till's position in the house was all-important; and position was dear to her. Long ago Matchem had taught her to "value her place", and that became her rule of life. (*SSG* 219)

Cather could have made good use of the above passage to elaborate on what Morrison calls the "historical discourse on slave parent-child relationships and pain" (1992: 22). Yet Cather evades the direct confrontation of slavery; instead, she focuses on the ways how slavery affects the people in her drama.

In Bernice Slote's view, Cather's imaginative world is one of subtle human relationships in settings of extraordinary physical reality (1986: ix). As far as *Sapphira and the Slave Girl* is concerned, the novel is about the subtle relationships among different family members and within the whole neighborhood of Back Creek. A key to the understanding of these relationships is slavery. Within the household of the Colberts, Sapphira is the only person who takes for granted her ownership of the body and soul of her slaves. Working alongside the slave men he oversees, Henry, on the other hand, has always doubted the rightness of owning slaves. When Sapphira passes away, he liberates all of his wife's slaves and takes a lot of trouble to help them find good places. If their different standpoint on slavery is only one of the many reasons for the discord between the husband and the wife, the conflict between Rachel and her mother is largely caused by their different attitudes towards slavery. Even when she was a child, Rachel deemed the owning of slaves wrong. Rachel hates her mother's voice in sarcastic reprimand to the slaves (*SSG* 137). Rachel and Sapphira's relationship worsens when Rachel helps to set free her mother's slave Nancy. Outside the Colberts' household, the residents make clear distinctions between the white and the colored, the Southerners and the Northerners. For instance, "none of the mountain boys will work along with colored hands" (*SSG* 81) for even the poorest whites consider themselves high above the slaves. Within the whites, the schoolmaster, the priest David Fairhead, and the postmistress Mrs. Bywaters are "Northerners" at heart. Both Rachel and Mr. Whitford (the carpenter and coffin-maker of Back Creek) are pro-abolitionists.

Even though *Sapphira and the Slave Girl* is set in slave-holding Virginia, Cather's focus in her last novel is not primarily on slavery itself. In "Light on Adobe Walls"[①], Cather maintains that "no art can do anything at all with great natural forces or great elemental emotions. No poet can write of love, hate, jealousy. He can only touch these things as they affect the people in his drama and his story" (*WCW* 124-125). In *Sapphira and the Slave Girl*, instead of dealing directly with a topic as heavy as slavery or economic structures, Cather's main concern is about the effect they have exerted on the everyday life of the neighborhood of Back Creek. In this way, Cather tells the truth about all the important issues that are related to daily life, but she tells them in the way as Emily Dickinson implies, "Tell the truth but tell it slant."

## 2.2 Propriety and Sexuality in the Neighborhood of *Shadows on the Rock* and *A Lost Lady*

In *Sapphira and the Slave Girl*, even though slavery is not the central thematic concern of Cather, it is one of the major determinants of what constitute the main plot of the novel. In *Shadows on the Rock*, published during the Great Depression, Cather seems to throw out of the window all the elements that other writers of the 1930s deem worthwhile to write about, and to concentrate instead on the goings on of the everyday life of "an orderly little French household" (*WCW* 16) in a remote

---

① "Light on Adobe Walls" was not published during Cather's life time and it was collected in *Willa Cather on Writing*.

community. The setting of *Shadows on the Rock* is the French colony Quebec between 1697 and 1698. The French household of the pharmacist Euclid Auclair and his twelve-year-old daughter Cécile form the core of that Quebecois community. It is from their domestic life that readers get a vantage point to what has happened in the whole community. Outside of the domesticity, clashes and political conflicts do exist, yet they are not as significant as the quiet domestic life led by the father and the daughter.

Chronologically speaking, *Shadows on the Rock* is Cather's tenth novel. Its thematic concern, very much like that of *Obscure Destinies*, is precisely about daily-ness itself—the specific and intensely local practices that make up everyday life (Milington, 1999: 30). At the moment of its initial publication, this story did not win as much favor as Cather's former works had. For the topics she dealt with in both *Shadows on the Rock* and *Obscure Destinies*, Cather was taken to task by Granville Hicks for writing works that fall into "supine romanticism" (1967: 147) and encourage escapism from the problems of modern life. Later, in 1937, Lionel Trilling in the *New Republic* wrote extremely negative views on Cather's later works. In Trilling's opinion, Cather's concern with "pots and pans" does not seem much more than an oblique defense of gentility and Cather's latest books consist chiefly of an irritated exclusion of those elements of modern life (1980: 66-67).

These two critics' views exert great impact on the reception of this book. In the words of Rosowski, *Shadows on the Rock* has received less enthusiastic attention than most of Cather's other fictions and it is one of Cather's least discussed novels (1988: 62). In China, no single essay is devoted to the interpretation of this novel; nor has there been a Chinese translation version of this story so far.[①] A study of the

---

[①] In China, the 1980s and the late 1990s as well as the years around 2010 are three important periods in the translation of Willa Cather's works. With the exception of *Alexander's Bridge,* all of Cather's novels are translated into Chinese; some of them even get more than one version. Most of Cather's short stories get their Chinese version. Compared with the attention to the novels and short stories, Cather's novella get less attention from scholars. Among them, only *A Lost Lady* was translated into Chinese in 2010, others like *My Mortal Enemy*, *Shadows on the Rock*, *Lucy Gayheart* and *Sapphira and the Slave Girl* as well have not been translated so far.

depiction of the neighborhood in this novel from the perspective of everyday life can throw new lights on the understanding of this novel and promote a fair reevaluation of this novel.

Unlike what she has done in her previous works, in *Shadows on the Rock*, Cather delineates in detail the town the Auclairs inhabit at the very beginning of the book:

> Divest your mind of Oriental color, and you saw here very much such a mountain rock, cunningly built over with churches, convents, fortifications, gardens, following the natural irregularities of the headland on which they stood; some high, some low, some thrust up on a spur, some nestling in a hollow, some sprawling unevenly along a declivity. (*LN* 466)

Readers can tell easily from Cather's description that the social and the political world of Quebec City in the seventeenth century is scarcely a democratic one. Instead, the whole neighborhood is a hierarchy well symbolized in the verticality of its settings (Stout, 2000: 255). To be sure, Quebec is not Cather's first town pervaded with hierarchical systems. Not coincidentally, Moonstone in *The Song of the Lark* shares many similarities with Quebec. In Moonstone, even the children are fully aware of the fact that the social classifications of their town conform to certain topographical boundaries:

> To the west of this street (the main business street) lived all the people "in society". Sylvester Street, the third parallel with Main Street on the west, was the longest in town, and the best dwellings were built along it... The Methodist Church was in the center of the town, facing the court-house square... In the part of Moonstone that lay east of Main Street, toward the deep ravine which, farther south, wound by Mexican Town, lived all the humble citizens, the people who voted but did not run for office. (*NS* 320)

In Quebec, all the social and religious elites, like the count, the bishop and the nuns live on the peak while the poor or the disreputable live at the bottom of the rock. In Cather's words, "No one building on the rock was on the same level with any other"

## Chapter II The Practice of the Neighborhood

and "respectability stopped with the cobble-stones." (*NS* 466-503) Euclide Auclair, the apothecary of the town, lives midway on the Mountain Hill, which is the one and only thoroughfare connecting the Upper Town with the Lower.

Occupying the advantage of being close to the Upper Town and the Lower, the Auclairs maintain a good relationship with almost all the members of the town. They have a relationship of mutual dependence with the social elites of the town: Count Frontenac, Euclid's patron and the Governor General of Canada, Bishop Laval, the nuns, Mother Juschereau in particular, and the rich fur-trader Pierre Charron. In addition, they pay visits to the Pommiers (a cobbler family) and the Pigeons (a baker family) on a regular basis. They also keep an eye on Jacques, a prostitute's six-year-old son, and help out the outcast Blinker.

Thematically, *Shadows on the Rock* is the story of how the inhabitants of Quebec, the Auclairs in particular, sustain life there. Far away from the culture that has shaped both their sense of self and their world, the early Quebecois are faced with the challenge of how to transform the strange world into a familiar one. Madame Auclair was an expert in maintaining the same lifestyle as they lived in Paris even after they moved to this crude land. All the colonists in Quebec liked to drop in at Euclide Auclair's house upon the slightest pretext, for the interior of his house was like home to the Frenchborn (*SR* 477). Madame Auclair's successful housekeeping has much to do with all the beautiful objects she has brought with her from France: the carpet, the dining table, the arm chairs and sofa, the window curtains, the candelabra and china shepherd boy sitting on the mantel, the color prints of pastoral scenes, the fine linen, feather beds and coverlids and down pillows. More importantly, her successful housekeeping has much to do with her attention and adherence to the sense of "our way" of conducting everyday life (*SR* 479).

To maintain "our way" of lifestyle, the Auclairs must follow strictly the social norms of order and propriety. Only under the condition that propriety and order are observed, can they distinguish their way of life from that of the others'. In Cather's story, propriety and order are clearly not only objective features of an elegant way of living, but are imbued with ethical and moral significance. To live one's life orderly and properly is so significant that Madame Auclair exhorts her daughter with these words, "without order our lives would be disgusting, like those of the poor savages". (*SR* 479) In *Shadows on the Rock*, for their adherence to the morals of propriety and order in their everyday life, both Madame Auclair and her daughter regard themselves spiritually superior to other residents of their neighborhood.

When Madame Auclair tries to inculcate the sense of "our way" in her daughter, she largely attributes her successful management of her home much to the ethical superiority of their nationality—"At home, in France, we have learned to do all these things in the best way, and we are conscientious, and that is why we are called the most civilized people in Europe and other nations envy us" (*SR* 479). Yet what she fails to realize and point out for her daughter is that in real life, the practice of propriety also has much to do with one's economic circumstances.

While Madame Auclair is blind to the big difference between being privileged and poor, the author is not. In her letter to Governor Wilbur Cross of Connecticut, Cather confessed that she found the life the characters in the book live admirable, yet there was "a kind of feeling, about life and human fate" (*WCW* 15) she could not wholly accept. In *Shadows on the Rock*, from time to time, Cather warns us of the limitations of the Auclairs' understanding of culture. Since Cécile can be very judgmental about the lifestyle of the people beneath her, Cather keeps reminding readers of the dangers of aligning with Cécile. For instance, when Cécile, together with Pierre Charron, pays a visit to the Harnois, she finds everything there, "the cooking, eating, sleeping, living", repulsive (*SR* 586). The four daughters of the Harnois tumble into a dirty bed with their legs badly bitten by mosquitoes and they dry their faces with a common towel. Influenced by her mother's opinion, and based on what her prejudiced eyes could detect, Cécile imputes the loss of order and propriety to the Harnois' lousiness. Yet readers are aware of the fact that back at the Auclairs' house, they have eucalyptus balls, which are sent to her father from France every year (*SR* 585). Details such as this testify to the importance of one's social and economic status for the maintenance of one's proper manners.

In Pierre Mayol's analysis of the everyday life in the neighborhood, he lays much emphasis on the importance for each dweller to adhere to a system of values and behaviors and of a "knowing-how-to-live-with" in the practice of the neighborhood (qtd. in de Certeau et al., 1998: 16-17). Among all the inhabitants of Quebec, Jacques Gaux and his mother live in the Lower Town, thus occupying a very low status in the neighborhood. Yet they understand quite well the importance of behaving well in the neighborhood. In *Shadows on the Rock*, Jacques is characterized as a very precocious boy. He is four-year-old yet he seems to be aware of his place all the time. He never tells lies, he tries to be clean and he is devoted to Cécile and her father (*SR* 496). He is also well aware of the fact that he and his mother fall into to a different social group than that of Cécile. Jacques is very fond of Cécile's silver cup, yearning for the same security and privileges symbolized by the cup. He regards the cup with "respectful, wistful admiration", and "before the milk or chocolate was poured, he like[s] to hold it and trace with his finger-tips the letters that made it so peculiarly and almost sacredly hers" (*SR* 520). Much as Jacques longs for the privilege enjoyed by his patroness, he declines Cécile's offer to drink coffee from her cup. Jacques never steps beyond the role he is expected to perform. His good behavior yields a "profit" (qtd. in de Certeau et al., 1998: 8)—he is a welcome guest in the Auclairs, and he is also rewarded with a pair of new shoes from the Governor.

The same is true with Jacques's mother, 'Toinette. 'Toinette is an arrogant, but much-despised woman in the neighborhood. Yet even she knows perfect well that there are social norms that she should not offend. After showing her impertinence in the face of Auclair by accusing him of meddling in her family affair, 'Toinette "wished she had been more civil"; so that she might get a reward of "some chocolate" (*SR* 521). On another occasion, when she is found out to have left her son wandering on the street on a cold night, 'Toinette loses her nerve faced with the thunder from the bishop. She knew that the bishop was serious by saying that he would take the child and put him with the Sisters of the Congregation if she dared to neglect her duty once again. She is conscious of the fact that poor and notorious as she is, she cannot afford the heavy price she would have to pay if she dared to challenge the authority represented by the bishop. Hence, she locks her son within the house all the rest of the winter, and never goes out herself unless she has another person keep an eye on him.

Jacques and his mother are not the only socially humble inhabitants who follow strictly the rule of propriety in the neighborhood. When Blinker comes for the soup in the Auclairs, he tries to behave as well as he can. Despite his eagerness for the soup, Blinker manages not to make any noise— "He knew it distressed Cécile if he gurgled his soup" (*SR* 472). Also he understands that if he does not show caution, he might humiliate himself and even worse, he might be deprived of the chance of having a bowl of soup in the Auclairs' home. If Jacques and Blinker are instances of being rewarded for coping well with the regulations of propriety in the neighborhood, in *Shadows on the Rock*, the episode of a girl named Marie is an opposite example of how people going against propriety are punished by the neighborhood. In *Shadows on the Rock*, Cather does not specify what kind of crime or to what extent Marie has offended the neighborhood, yet she does point out the severe consequences caused by her deviation: she is driven out by the town fellows, shunned by men and women alike and in the end, after her death, her corpse is "thrown into a ditch and buried like that of some unclean animal" (*SR* 487).

In terms of the year of publication, *A Lost Lady* comes out seven years earlier than *Shadows on the Rock*. If the major thematic concern of *Shadows on the Rock* is about how Cécile and people around her carry out the social norm of propriety in the neighborhood, *A Lost Lady* is about a young man's disillusion with the titular lady, Mrs. Forrester's transgression against the norm of propriety in the neighborhood. Like Quebec in *Shadows on the Rock*, in *A Lost Lady*, Sweet Water, the little town in which both Niel (the young man) and Mrs. Forrester live, is also a hierarchical one. The demarcation line among each social stratum is quite clear-cut.

In *A Lost Lady*, even the little boys know they are expected to act differently when faced with the social elite. Whenever they come across Mrs. Forrester on their way to the picnic, the children single George Adams out as their representative to talk to her. George is singled out because every kid knows that Mrs. Forrester is a regular visitor in his house (*ALL* 15), which indicates the fact that they are of the same social class. To various degrees, almost all the children are conscious of the fact that Mrs. Forrester is special. Coming from the lowest social stratum, the Blum brothers know much better than their companions that such fortunate and privileged class represented by Mrs. Forrester is an axiomatic fact in the social order (*ALL* 19).

## Chapter II The Practice of the Neighborhood

When Niel fell from the tree and was carried to Mrs. Forrester's house, the other boys entered her house, but the Blum brothers "knew their place was outside the kitchen door" (*ALL* 26).

According to Pierre Mayol, the word propriety is used to designate the code that guides the presentation of one's body in public (qtd. in de Certeau et al., 1998: 16). The code works not because it is put down in black and white, but because it is understood and internalized by all dwellers. In the story, when Adolph Blum, the son of the German tailor, happens to find out the adultery committed between Mrs. Forrester and Ellinger, he is fully aware that what she does is against the principle of propriety. However, the fact that Mrs. Forrester belongs to the privileged class of the rich and fortunate while Adolph who belongs to the lower class turns this scandal into another matter. Instead of accusing Mrs. Forrester of offending the rule of propriety, the little boy finds excuses for her misdemeanor—"these warm-blooded, quick-breathing people took chances" (*ALL* 68).

From this, one can extrapolate the important role both the economic and political factors play in deciding whether one is acting properly or improperly. Before her husband goes bankrupt, whatever Mrs. Forrester does is considered not only proper but superior to all the other women do in the neighborhood — "compared with her, other women were heavy and dull; even the pretty ones seemed lifeless" (*ALL* 41). In other words, if Mrs. Forrester is just one common housewife, her behavior of coming out "in her apron, waving a buttery iron spoon, or shook [shaking] cherry-stained fingers at the new arrival" (*ALL* 12) would be regarded as improper act. But since she is Mrs. Forrester, whatever she chooses to do, it is regarded as "lady-like". The admiring middle-aged men who visit her home cannot imagine her in any dress or situation in which she would not be charming (*ALL* 13). Since wealth is in constant flux and flow, once Mrs. Forrester's economic situation worsens, she would be deprived of the privilege she formerly enjoys. Those past glories only make her an easy target for harsh criticism from the townspeople. When Niel finds for the first time the relationship between Mrs. Forrester and Ellinger, he judges her behavior harshly, "lilies that fester smell far worse than weeds". (*ALL* 87)

It is interesting to note the big difference in attitudes that Mrs. Forrester's behavior has triggered in Niel and Adolph Blum. Niel acts much more irritated towards Mrs. Forrester's adultery for he and Mrs. Forrester belong to the same social class, which makes him feel entitled to pass judgment on her behavior. Adolph acts much more tolerant towards Mrs. Forrester's behavior for he comes from a fairly humble background. In addition, poor people like him sometimes have to rely upon rich people like Mrs. Forrester for their livelihood. When Adolph comes to the back door with his fish, Mrs. Forrester never haggles about the price, nor does she give him away when she buys games from him in the closed season (*ALL* 68).

The importance of wealth to the maintenance of propriety in the story can also be witnessed in the neighbors' attitude towards the Forresters' residence. Before the Forresters become impoverished, their house is regarded by the town people as the most pleasant house at Sweet Water and everyone longs to go inside and have a look. After the captain becomes ill and helpless, the place is invaded by the gossipy women in the town. To their dismay, they find that "they had been fooled all these years. There was nothing remarkable about the place at all! The kitchen was inconvenient, the sink was smelly. The carpets were worn, the curtains faded, the clumsy, old-fashioned furniture they wouldn't have had for a gift, and the upstairs bed-rooms were full of dust and cobwebs" (*ALL* 138). The change of attitude towards the same matter further indicates the complexity of the mechanism of propriety.

Mrs. Forrester used to be a master of social manners when her husband was in the full flush of success. She could maintain her elegance and keep control of herself so long as she is Mrs. Forrester. Shortly after their misfortune had begun to fall upon them, faced with the inquisitive eyes of the town people, she had maintained her old reserve. Her smiling, careless manner defeats the efforts of all the inquisitive housewives from the town. "They still felt they must put on their best dress and carry a card-case when they went to the Forresters."(*ALL* 137) However, with the decline of Captain Forrester's wealth and influence, Mrs. Forrester is demystified. After getting the news of the marriage of her lover, Frank Ellinger, to a rich woman, Mrs. Forrester collapses. She leaves her sleeping husband behind to call Ellinger at a rainy night. At first, she manages to call up in the voice of "a woman, young, beautiful, happy, — warm and at her ease, sitting in her own drawing-room and talking on a stormy night to a dear friend far away" (*ALL* 133). But the strong sense of betrayal finally takes the upper hand—the words she says and the way she behaves herself overflow the boundary of propriety for a married woman. Without Niel's timely cut-off of the telephone line, her hysteria would be spread through the telephone and become the object of ridicule of the whole town.① Her later relationship and attitude toward the nouveau-riche Ivy Peters further evidences the fact that Mrs. Forrester is just as vulnerable as the other women, falling prey to sexual abuse.

## 2.3 "Dead" Neighborhood in *The Song of the Lark* and *The Professor's House*

Apart from the neighborhood discussed above, there is another kind of neighborhood in Cather's writings. Both Panther Canyon in *The Song of the Lark* and Cliff City in *The Professor's House* are "dead" neighborhoods where civilization no longer exists. Yet Thea Kronborg's and Tom Outland's personal contacts with life that used to be lived in these places give them enlightenment about art, faith, desire and religion. While Thea Kronborg's experiencing of the everyday life of bygone residents of Panther Canyon in *The Song of the Lark* deepens her understanding of the significance of the integration of art into everyday life, what Tom Outland discovers about the rock cities in *The Professor's House* extends his definition of civilization, history and his own place in it.

In terms of the year of publication, *The Song of the Lark* and *The Professor's House* remain ten years apart. At first glance, there is hardly anything in common between these two stories. Whereas the former is set in various places, from mid-west small town Moonstone to big city Chicago, Southwest Arizona, Germany and then back to America again, charting the artistic growth of a young girl's rise from obscurity to fame as an opera singer, the focus of the latter is on the midlife crisis

---

① So much is involved in Cather's seemingly passing reference to Mrs. Forrester use of the telephone. According to Honor McKitrick Wallace's interpretation, Mrs. Forrester takes a great risk by choosing telephone to convey her strong feelings to her lover, and by doing so, she may expose her personal affairs to the public and thus become the object of gossip.

of Professor Godfrey St. Peter, resulting from the conflict between his disposition and the demands of people around him. Yet there are indeed great similarities shared between these two works. Linda De Roche asserts that the thematic concerns of the two stories are almost of the same kind: in *The Professor's House*, Cather gives a full illustration of the theme of unavoidable disappointments and disillusionment that result from comprised ideals she has developed in *The Song of the Lark*. Furthermore, in both stories, Cather experiments with the form of the novel. *The Song of the Lark* is described by both Robin Heyeck and James Woodress as "overstuffed, going on and on" (1979: 651). Cather says in a letter to a friend that in *The Professor's House*, she means to create the impression of Professor Godfey St. Peter's house rather overcrowded and stuffy with new things (*WCW* 31). In the following section of this chapter, this book is going to explore Cather's depiction of the lifestyle of ancient residents in these two works. Both Part Four "The Ancient People" of *The Song of the Lark* and Part Two "Tom Outland's Story" of *The Professor's House* are based on Cather's two-month journey to Arizona and New Mexico in the spring of 1912.

Feeling exhausted by her demanding duties in *McClure's*, Cather went to Winslow, Arizona in the spring of 1912, to pay a visit to her brother Douglass, who was working with the Santa Fe Railroad during that period. Accompanied by her brother, Cather explored the native American ruins, the sleeping canyons and rocky cliff dwellings in the Southwest. For Cather, the highlight of this visit is a trip to Walnut Canyon, a cliff-dwelling site near Flagstaff that would be designated as a national monument in 1915.

The 1912 journey plays an important role in Cather's twinned regional and literary trajectories (Halverson, 2013: 136). Before Cather travels to Arizona and New Mexico, encountering another alien landscape that needs to be translated into language, she does not know what to do with the vast expanses of sky and earth of her hometown. Her first novel *Alexander's Bridge* is basically "the result of meeting some interesting people in London" and is very like "what painters call a studio picture" (*WCW* 91). What she sees and does in the Southwest saves her from the drawing room conventions. In other words, this southwest trip energizes Cather's imagination and it rekindles her interest in her home state of Nebraska as eligible literary material. When Cather comes back east after several months from the west, she is ready to produce her second "first" novel *O Pioneers!*, which is a story about some Scandinavians and Bohemians, who have been neighbors of her childhood. The novel was published in the year of 1913 and turned out to be a tremendous success. Two years after the publication of this novel, Cather published *The Song of the Lark*. In this book, the place where Thea Kronborg, the heroine of the story has her epiphany is set in Walnut Canyon, Arizona, which is the very place modeled on Cather's 1912 trip.

Cather enjoys this trip very much. In one of her letters from that time, she wrote, "It (the three days in the upper Canyons—Clear Creek, Jack's Canyon and Chevelin) had all the advantages of a camping trip and yet we got home every night and had hot baths and beds to sleep in. We stared every morning at day light, light wagon and light camp outfits, canteens, coffee, bacon, fruit, cream, etc." (*SL* 157) Cather's enthusiasm for her camping trip reflects a national vogue for outdoor life at the turn of the century. Yet, this kind of outdoor activity is not available to everyone in the whole society. Instead, camping and other forms of vigorous outdoor recreation are loaded with gender, class and racial significance and vacations like Cather's are a traditionally masculine, upper-class experience newly available to the middle class (Halverson, 2013: 137).

In *The Song of the Lark*, Thea's opportunity to take a trip to Arizona is offered by her wealthy suitor Frederick Ottenburg, the "beer prince", who is the head of the Chicago branch of his family's brewing business. Although it seems that Thea takes good care of herself during her excursions to Panther Canyon and its cliff-dwelling ruins (Cather's fictional rendition of Walnut Canyon), without help from Frederick and the foreman of the Arizona ranch, Old Henry Biltmer, Thea's trip would hardly have been possible. Frederick sends Thea to Arizona to recuperate her spirits following a bout of tonsillitis, which reflects the popularity of "camp cures" at the turn of the twentieth century. In Thea's case, the camping experience offers both escape and relief from daily competitions; it also gives her a chance for deep introspection. Apart from "camp cures", another important reason for the popularity of this outdoor recreation is that it "give(s) modern Americans a sense of replicating a more authentic, primitive lifestyle" (*SL* 137). In the case of Cather's fiction, it gives the explorers a chance to get nearer to the everyday life of bygone residents, the Indians, to be specific.

The everyday life of bygone residents does not simply unfold itself to its viewers. The explorers need to be persons with acute inward perception so as to find identification with the life of those old inhabitants. Thea Kronborg, for instance, is such a qualified explorer:

> On the first day that Thea climbed the water trail she began to have intuitions about the woman who had worn the path, and who had spent so great a part of their lives going up and down it. She found herself trying to walk as they must have walked, with a feeling in her feet and knees and loins which she had never known before — which must have come up to her out of the accustomed dust of that rocky trail. She could feel the weight of an Indian baby hanging to her back as she climbed. (*EN* 550)

Before Thea arrives at Panther Canyon, she is surrounded by artists with whom she has great difficulty identifying. Her voice lesson teacher "liked her for whatever was least admirable in her" (*EN* 511). Other singers seem to care more for money than true art and the audiences are too ignorant to make distinctions between a true talent and a fake one. Thea is stuck on her way to artistic success. The experience of living among the ruins of ancient Indians not only liberates her from the grinding and fruitless music lessons in Chicago, but also helps her find a sense of belonging. She feels more connected to other women—she finds herself walking the same way as those ancient women and she even imagines herself carrying a baby as she climbs the cliff.

Before her encounter with Panther Canyon, Thea only has a vague idea about what she is going to do with her career. The trip somehow helps her unify and resolve her inner conflicts. As she follows the ancient trails in Panther Canyon and explores the ruins of the ancient residents, Thea recovers her "strength of purpose" (de Roche, 2006: 95). One morning, as she was standing upright in the pool, splashing water between her shoulder-blades with a big sponge, Thea had an epiphany "what was any

## Chapter II The Practice of the Neighborhood

art but an effort to make a sheath, a mould in which to imprison for a moment the shining, elusive element which is life itself… The Indian women had held it in their jars… In singing, one made a vessel of one's throat and nostrils and held it on one's breath, caught the stream in a scale of natural interval" (*EN* 552). In other words, after seeing those fragments of pottery, Thea could make an analogy between her own art and those of Indian women's. The ancient potter's dedication to art regardless of the utilitarian purpose of these vessels provokes Thea to dedicate herself to the same ideal. She can't help saluting endeavor, achievement, desire, glorious striving of human art! Exalted by the enlightment, she makes up her mind to follow the steps of this vanished race of cliff dwellers. She realizes that true art is immortal because "along the trail, in the stream, under the spreading cactus, there still glittered in the sun the bits of their [the ancient people's] frail clay vessels, fragments of their [the ancient people's] desire" (*EN* 566).

In *The Song of the Lark*, apart from Thea's perspective, the other details that are concerned with the daily life of the ancient cliff dwellers are unveiled from the perspective of Old Henry. From Old Henry, readers get to know that the division of labor in ancient times is quite clear—while men go hunting and provide food, women wait at home and find solutions to drinking water. The fragments left from the past indicate that the ancient people have developed masonry and pottery. Their craft skills are developed to such a degree that they reveal some secrets about the daily life of these ancient people to the modern viewers. Some of the pottery is decorated in different colors, in graceful geometrical patterns, which is a good indicator of these ancient people's strong sense of beauty. The "crested serpent's head, painted in red on terra-cotta" (*EN* 553) found on a fragment of a shallow bowl may have something to do with the tribe's religious totem. That is what Cather informs readers of the everyday life of the ancient cliff dwellers. In *The Song of the Lark,* Cather's emphasis weighs more on the impact of the ruins of these ancient people on Thea than anything else—how it inspires her to find her deep longings, to find justification for that kind of longing, and further still how to pluck up her courage to devote herself to music as well.

Thea's time in Panther Canyon anticipates, to some degree, Tom Outland's sojourn on the Blue Mesa in another of Cather's mesa novels, *The Professor's House* (Williams, 2005: 162). *The Professor's House* is about the mid-life crisis of Professor Godfrey St. Peter, who is a sensitive and intelligent man. Yet somewhat surprisingly, the novel has its genesis not in the professor's story but in his brilliant student—Tom Outland (de Roche, 2006: 136). Two years after Cather's 1912 trip to the Southwest, Cather, accompanied by her friend, Edith Lewis, made a second trek into the Southwest's high mesas, a landscape that clearly "touched a chord in her" (*EN* 136). This time, their weeks of exploration of ancient cliff dwellings, including an unexcavated cliff village, climaxes with a sensational experience, during which the friends, lost in uncharted territory, were left to fend for themselves while their guide went in search of help (de Roche, 2006: 137). Immediately after their return from that journey, Cather composed a story, the main plot of which derives directly from the experience of that incident. The tale is named "The Blue Mesa". The tale itself remains unfinished yet its main plot is transplanted seven years later into the middle part of *The Professor's House*, under the name of "Tom Outland's Story".

"Tom Outland's Story" is a narrative complete in itself, yet its placement—the center of the novel's three-book structure, makes all too obvious its significance to the entire book. Thematically, this part solves the mystery of the mysterious young man's history and character (de Roche, 2006: 141). When Tom is a call boy in Pardee, New Mexico, he happens to befriend Roddy Blake, a rough-and-ready railroad fireman, who takes good care of him when he catches pneumonia that winter. For the sake of Tom's health, Blake gives up his former job and finds a berth for Tom and him with the Sitwell Cattle Company. Their duty is to "ride the range with a bunch of grass cattle all summer" (*PH* 112) near the Blue Mesa area, a geographical maze of seemingly impenetrable canyons and impregnable cliffs. The nearer they get to the Blue Mesa, the more tantalizing the Blue Mesa becomes for them. What follows is the group's adventure story in the Blue Mesa. Like all the other adventure stories, Cather's adventure story contains moments of excitement, disappointment and betrayal, yet unlike the others, it also depicts moments of peacefulness, during which Cather reveals to readers the remnants of an extinct civilization.

Compared with her portrayal of the daily life of the ancient people in *The Song of the Lark*, Cather's depiction of the everyday life of the residents of Cliff City in *The Professor's House* is more concrete and all-embracing. The overall impression the city gives is its being "as still as sculpture" (*PH* 122). All the dwelling places are hung together as if they had a kind of composition: "pale little houses of stone nestling close to one another, perched on top of each other, with flat roofs, narrow windows, straight walls, and in the middle of the group, a round tower" (*PH* 122). As far as the tower is concerned, "there was something symmetrical and powerful about the swell of the masonry" (*PH* 122). The tower itself indicates its designers are people with a feeling for design. Tom and his partners' findings uncover almost all the significant aspects of the practice of the everyday life of the ancient residents.

In addition to this introduction to the architectural styles of the ancients, Cather also depicts in detail the ways how these ancient people conducted their daily life. These ancient people had developed their agriculture and animal husbandry for "there were corncobs everywhere, and ears of corn with the kernels still on them…We found dried beans, too, and strings of pumpkin seeds, and plum seeds, and…turkey bones"(*PH* 125). The other aspects that are revealed to readers include the way how they did their cooking: "it was evidently a kind of common kitchen, where they roasted and baked and probably gossiped" (*PH* 127); how they dressed themselves up: "we found clothes; yucca moccasins, and what seemed like cotton cloth, woven in black and white. Never any wool, but sheepskins tanned with the fleece on them" (*PH* 130); the extent to which they developed their craft (there are beautifully shaped water jars, grinding stones and several clay ovens) and their medical conditions as well (Tom and his friends found a deerskin bag full of little tools, which contained a number of surgical instruments; a stone lancet, a bunch of fine bone needles, wooden forceps, and a catheter) (*PH* 129).

The study of the remains of these daily life objects, be it "yucca-fibre mats, charred bones and charcoal, or a deerskin bag full of little tools" (*PH* 127-129) is so significant that they tell stories to the later visitors about the history and culture of that particular group during certain historical period. For Tom and his friends, to explore Cliff City is to piece together what has happened in the distant past. After seeing the tower, Tom says he can draw a conclusion that the people who built this tower must have had a strong sense of proportion. From the intactness of the water jars and bowls they find, they extrapolate the fact that this village has never been ransacked by an enemy. Also the residents of Cliff City do not build their town in a hurry, which can be told from the care they take in designing their houses:

> The cedar joists had been felled with stone axes and rubbed smooth with sand. The little poles that lay across them and held up the clay floor of the chamber above, were smoothly polished. The door lintels were carefully fitted (the doors were stone slabs held in place by wooden bars fitted into hasps). The clay dressing that covered the stone walls was tinned, and some of the chambers were frescoed in geometrical patterns, one color laid on another. In one room was a painted border, little tents, like Indian tepees, in brilliant red. (*PH* 129)

Even though the inhabitants who used to inhabit Cliff City are no longer there by the time Tom and his friends took a trip to their village, the fine arrangement of their dwelling place composes a life narrative, which speaks louder than words about the civilization and disposition of Cliff City dwellers (qtd. in de Certeau et al., 1998: 145).

In *The Song of the Lark*, it is mainly through Thea's perspective that we readers get a glimpse of the everyday life of those bygone residents. In *The Professor's House*, in contrast, Cather offers us both Tom's and Father Duchene's interpretation of the practice of the everyday life of these bygone Indian groups. For his acute inward perception, Tom is capable of giving a detailed description about what he and his friend have found. Yet he has great difficulty in interpreting his findings due to his lack of knowledge and narrow field of vision. It is from the perspective of Father Duchene that Cather recreates the complexity of the life and death of this ancient tribe:

> They lived for something more than food and shelter. They had an appreciation of comfort, and went even further than that.
>
> ...
>
> They developed physically and improved in the primitive arts. They had looms and

mills, and experimented with dyes. At the same time, they possibly declined in the arts of war, in brute strength and ferocity.

...

They were probably wiped out, utterly exterminated, by some roving Indian tribe without culture or domestic virtues, some horde that fell upon them in their summer camp and destroyed them for their hides and clothing and weapons, or from mere love of slaughter. (*PH* 134-135)

Father Duchene's interpretation also gives significance to the corpse of Mother Eve. When Tom and his friends find out the corpse of Mother Eve, the details he observes convinces him that she must have been murdered by someone else: "there was a great wound in her side, the ribs stuck out through the dried flesh. Her mouth was open as if she were screaming" (*PH* 130). From the color of her hair and teeth, Tom and his friends suppose that she must have been quite young when she was murdered. That is all the story Tom and his friends could tell of Mother Eve. Compared with Tom's interpretation of the story of Mother Eve, Father Duchene's version is much more complicated and intriguing. Much as he likes the title Tom and his friends have given to Mother Eve, Father Duchene does not believe her death has anything to do with the destruction of her people. Instead, he considers her death a personal tragedy, the case of a woman being given a death penalty by her husband for her adultery.

Father Duchene's interpretation of what he has found in Mother Eve is tinted with the ugly side of the ancient society. For his naivety, much of Tom's perception of the everyday life of Cliff City dwellers is flooded with sunshine. From Tom's perspective, these old inhabitants lead a comfortable life: they have abundant supply of food and clothing; in addition, they are religious and artistic. By inserting the perspective of Father Duchene into the narrative of the everyday life of those bygone inhabitants, Cather manages to give an objective picture of the primitive lifestyle of these ancient people.

Much like Thea's experience in Panther Canyon, Tom undergoes "an existential transformation" during his stay in Cliff City (Ellwanger, 2012: 53). Tom's transformation can be detected from the change of his perceptions of his relationship to the mesa. Before he reaches the mesa, it remains to be a mysterious "neighbor" that keeps tantalizing his mind. "There is something stirring about finding evidences of human labor and care in the soil of an empty country," Tom said. He and his friend Blake wanted to be the first men up there, and to see what it was like on the other side of their dwelling place (*PH* 212-216). When the thought of conquering gains the upper hand, what Tom can perceive in the mesa is nothing but its physical form—its height being more than a thousand of feet, its sheer cliffs that fell from the summit to the plain, and its south flank, just across the river that indicates some chance of accessibility (*PH* 214).

Tom's attitude starts to change the moment he sets his foot on the mesa. He cannot repress his admiration for the majesty of the place as well as its inhabitants. More than once, he acknowledges his incapability in articulating the beauty of the mesa: "I wish I could tell you what I saw there, just as I saw it, on that first morning, through a veil of lightly falling snow... The falling snow flakes, sprinkling the pinons, gave it a special kind of solemnity. I can't describe it" (*PH* 221). The closer Tom comes to the mesa, the more intimate his relationship with the place becomes. Being situated on the mesa enables him to experience his surroundings in a new bodily way (Ellwanger, 2012: 58). Having overcome the strict visual observation which has defined his first experience with the mesa, Tom begins to feel the place. He confesses that he has never breathed in anything that tasted so pure as the air in that valley and never had he tasted water as cold as ice, and so pure as what he has on the mesa (*PH* 220-226). During Tom's stay on the mesa, not only his sense of taste and sight is sharpened, but also his sense of beauty is activated. The numerous adjectives and nouns he uses to describe the setting as well as the everyday objects he has found on the mesa, such as "symmetrical and powerful, beautifully proportioned and solemnity" and the like, indicate that he is making great progress in responding with physically sensuousness to beauty.

Nevertheless, Tom's metamorphosis has not been accomplished until he parts with his friend Blake and is left alone on the mesa. Tom terminates his partnership with Blake because the latter sells out all the relics they have found during Tom's absence. Tom judges Blake's betrayal harshly, not because he feels morally superior to Blake but because one part of himself is just as acquisitive as Blake. In response to Tom's criticism, Blake reminds him about how they used to talk of "getting big money from the Government" (*PH* 247). Tom grudgingly admits that he had hoped that they would be paid for their work, and maybe "get a bonus of some kind" (*PH* 247) for their discovery. Tom feels compelled to drive Blake out of the mesa so that he could become a man of integrity. It's only after Tom extricates himself from all those monetary concerns that he could see the mesa as a whole. Tom records his own metamorphosis in this way: "This was the first time I ever saw it as a whole… Something had happened in me that made it possible for me to co-ordinate and simplify… For me the mesa was no longer an adventure, but a religious emotion… It had formerly been mixed up with other motives; but now that they were gone, I had my happiness unalloyed" (*PH* 250).

Long after his departure from the mesa, Tom recalls the significance of that summer to his life, "What that night began lasted all summer. I stayed on the mesa until November. It was the first time I'd ever studied methodically, or intelligently… I can scarcely hope that life will give me another summer like that one. It was my high tide."(*PH* 253) The fact that Tom identifies his time on the mesa as his "high tide" shows his belief in the superiority of that mode of existence (Ellwanger, 2012: 60). What Tom undergoes on the mesa also explains why he could embrace death passionately in the World War I and why Cather would let her hero die prematurely before the others would make a profit out of his invention.

As a writer deeply influenced by her surroundings, Cather has a strong sense of place. Throughout her life, Cather lived in or visited many places, many of which she wrote into her fiction. The settings of her stories range from Middleland Nebraska to Southwest Colorado and Arizona, Northeast Quebec and Grand Manan, South Virginia and even France. Among these different regions, what she writes about most is Red Cloud, Nebraska. But other places, such as her Virginia home, the places she visited more than once and took great delight in also occupy an important place in her writings. She attaches great importance to these places not because she intends to demonstrate the regional differences and to sketch local color but because they are her deepest emotional resources, and in them she embodies universal themes

(Slote, 1986: ix). In revealing the dynamics of family and the social system of the neighborhood of Back Creek in *Sapphira and the Slave Girl*, of Quebec in *Shadows on the Rock*, and of Sweet Water in *A Lost Lady*, this book demonstrates the interlocking of race, power, sexuality and geography in Cather's diverse neighborhoods. Both Thea's experience in Panther Canyon and Tom's memory of the Blue Mesa are based on Cather's journeys into the Southwest. Place, rather than societal structures, seems to be of more immediate concern to Cather in her two mesa novels. In investigating Thea's and Tom's life stories in association with the place as well as the lifestyles of the ancient people living in these places, Cather highlights the significance of these places to the initiation of these two characters.

# Chapter III
# Doing-cooking

Out of all everyday life activities, culinary practices situate themselves at the most rudimentary level, at the most necessary but the most unappreciated level. Doing-cooking is the medium for a basic, humble and persistent practice that is repeated day after day. Yet food is neither innocent nor neutral, as "eating is always much more than eating" (qtd. in de Certeau et al., 1998: 198). The regularity and mundanity of eating and cooking often conceal deep cultural meanings, for culinary activities have much to do with not only human beings' basic instincts to sustain life, but also with the fabric of relationships to others and to one's self.[①] For instance, food allows for an assortment of associations and attachments to be swallowed with it, and this assortment could range from the emotional (it is grandma's cookies or mom's apple pie) to the evocative, from the religious to the cultural (Cozzi, 2010: 4). Food is used extensively as a literary device in Willa Cather's fiction, and one of the most popular approaches to Cather's food has been cultural study. For example, food in Cather's fiction is read as an expression of cultural practice shared among or

---

[①] Culinary activities are of course only one of the many fields of everyday life in which interpersonal relationships can be analyzed. According to Lefebvre's definition of everyday life in *Critique of Everyday Life* (Volume 1), it is in everyday life that the sum total of relations that make the human—and every human being—a whole takes its shape and its form… the critique of everyday life studies human nature in its concreteness.

integrated into different social, ethical and regional groups; it is also a metaphor that shows her anxiety over the Americanization or modernization of society as a whole.

The main argument of this chapter is that Cather's treatment of foodways in her major works is an expression of thematic concerns salient throughout her literary career. Doing-cooking is traditionally held as the sphere of women and is usually relegated to a matter of no importance. Making an implicit challenge to the traditional association between gender and cooking, Cather elevates cooking to the status of art in some of her works, saving innumerable housewives from the anonymity. In others, including *The Song of the Lark*, *One of Ours*, *My Ántonia* and *The Professor's House*, Cather creates women characters who make up their minds to liberate themselves from the kitchen and male figures who are quite devoted to cooking, thus subverting traditional concepts of the relationship between gender and cooking. The call of the past is strong in Cather's delineation of food in her major works as exemplified in her short story "Neighbor Rosicky". Cather's characters follow strictly their own particular ways of cooking so as to make a distinction between their own culture and the culture of others', as in the case of the mutual mistrust shared between Mrs. Burden and Mrs. Shimerda in *My Ántonia*. In addition to the analysis of these culinary practices, the author of the present dissertation wants to argue that the "how, where and when" of eating in Cather's works is used by the writer to convey the social status of the eaters and to measure the stability of the world.

## 3.1 The Gendered Aspect of Doing-cooking

Departing from but not totally irrelevant to the traditional perspectives adopted by cultural critics, my study is to examine Cather's foodways[①] as represented in her fiction in light of the theories of everyday life put forward by Luce Giard.

---

[①] In social science, foodways are the cultural, social and economic practices related to the production and consumption of food. It often refers to the intersection of food in culture, traditions and history. Foodways in Roger L. and Linda K. Welsch's book *Cather's Kitchens* are set into ethnic and regional perspective. For instance, the Welsch contend that the echoes of ethnic foods are strong in Cather's work and the rural atmosphere in her menus. My study of foodways in Cather's work pays more attention to the cultural resonation of food in Cather's works.

## Chapter III Doing-cooking

Giard's study is more anthropologic in nature, and her findings are mostly based on her investigations conducted in a little French town. While Giard's model has not been developed for representation, it does provide a useful analytic model focused on the processes and practices of everyday life that are represented in literary texts. It is helpful to summarize Giard's points on doing-cooking before applying it to the study of the representation of food in Cather's works. Reading through Giard's part to *The Practice of Everyday Life: Living and Cooking* on the topic of doing-cooking, I identify the following points pertinent to my discussion:

> Since life (culinary) activities demand as much intelligence, imagination, and memory as those traditionally held as superior, such as music and weaving, they rightly make up one of the strong aspects of ordinary culture.
> 
> ...
> 
> The responsibility for culinary practices falls almost exclusively on women and... people judge this work to be repetitive and monotonous, devoid of intelligence and imagination.
> 
> ...
> 
> We do "our own style" of cooking, "our" cuisine, the way we used to do over there...Food thus becomes a veritable discourse of the past and a nostalgic narrative about the country, the region, the city, or the village where one was born. (qtd. in de Certeau et al., 1998: 151-156)

Points one and two are connected. First, Giard subverts the stereotypical ideas about culinary activities, regarding them as demanding as much intelligence, imagination and memory as those traditionally held as superior activities, such as music and weaving. In doing so, Giard does the same thing as other everyday life theorists do—save everyday life from becoming anonymous, and in the case of Giard, save culinary activities in particular. The personal context of Giard's model is important and suggests the connection between points one and two. Before she conducts her survey on doing-cooking, Giard recalls her experience as a female child: she used to consider the feminine savoir faire that presides over buying food, preparing it and organizing meals as elementary, conventional, and pedestrian and therefore a bit stupid (*WCP* 152). She had always preferred her room and her books to doing-cooking when she was a child. Despite her efforts to distance herself from the feminine savoir faire, Giard finds, one day, to her great surprise, that she had become "an heiress and guardian of women culinary culture without wanting to be one" (*WCP* 153).

Giard's reluctance to be an heiress of female culinary tradition has much to do with the lower place that is given to culinary activities. These are held to be the domain of housewives, who can only handle housework while their husbands and sons earn their wages outside of the home. What housewives do day after day is commonly considered repetitive, tedious and time-consuming. This work forms a sharp contrast with the characteristics of men's work (intelligence-demanding, interesting, exciting, professional). Naturally, the initial reaction of a new female intellectual coming from a new generation, like Giard, is to feel compelled to alienate herself from such female culture. Only little by little, does she realize the difficulty of getting rid of such rich female heritage; it creeps into her marrow, slips past her mind's surveillance without her awareness. Seeing the futility of struggling against the impact of her heritage, Giard happily accepts the bequest from her female ancestors. Giard's changing attitude towards culinary activities—in her childhood, she tried to keep a distance from her mother's kitchen; in her adulthood, she considers culinary activities as significant as other forms of artistic creation—forms a parallel with Cather's attitude.

It is true that on more than one occasion Cather spoke highly of cooking. Food and cooking are often elevated to the status of art in her writings: "I have never found any intellectual excitement more intense than I used to feel when I spent a morning with one of these pioneer women at her baking or butter-making... My mind and stomach are one! I think and work with whatever it is that digests... No nation has ever produced great art that has not made a high art of cookery, because art appeals primarily to the senses... Art thrives best where the personal life is richest, fullest and warmest, from the kitchen up."(*WCP* 10-149)

However, for a long period, like Giard as a child, Cather is constantly on guard against her female tradition. She dressed like a boy in her childhood and she aspired to become a scientist when she enrolled at university. During her apprenticeship years, she modeled her writing on male writers instead of female ones. It is works by Virgil, John Bunyan, Leo Tolstoy, Gustave Flaubert, and Henry James that seem to have left the deepest imprint on her mind. Indeed, she seems to have no high opinion of women writers. From 1895 to 1899, she voiced her negative views on women writings in journals like *Nebraska State Journal, the Lincoln Courier* and *Pittsburgh Leader* more than once. "Sometimes I wonder why God ever trust [literary] talent in the hands of women, they usually make such an infernal mess of it," she wrote in 1895. "I think He must do it as a sort of ghastly joke." (*KA* 408) In Cather's opinion, women writers, poetesses in particular, have only been successful in poetry of the most highly subjective nature, and if a woman writes any poetry at all worth reading, it must be "emotional in the extreme, self-centered, self-absorbed" (*KA* 348). Under such circumstances, both women poets' and novelists' subject matter are limited and superficial; all they could write about is love: "They have a sort of sex consciousness that is abominable" (*KA* 409). Cather also laments Kate Chopin's waste of her gifts on "so trite and sordid a theme" as adultery in *The Awakening*. Nor does she give a high appraisal to Harriet Beecher Stowe's *Uncle Tom's Cabin,* simply for the reason that it is the embodiment of the feminine mind "hankering for hobbies and missions" (*KA* 406). Women for Cather seem to use art rather than to make it: "Has any woman ever really had the art instinct, the art necessity? Is it not with them a substitute, a transferred enthusiasm, an escape valve for what has sought or is seeking another channel?" (*KA* 158).

To find reasons for Cather's negative comments on women writers during this period, one needs to take the literary culture during which Cather received her apprenticeship into account. Even though the majority of Cather's works were composed in the period from the 1910s to the 1930s, her artistic training began much earlier. In the opinion of John H. Randall III, "Cather grew to literary awareness in the eighteen-nineties; it was the nineties that shaped her artistic consciousness, and she remained a child of the nineties for the rest of her life." (1960: 1) In his book, *The Landscape and the Looking Glass*, Randall listed out the impact of two cultural movements, namely, "Art for Art's Sake" and "The Populist Movement" on Cather's formulation of artistic principles. What he failed to mention is the gendered side of the cultural atmosphere of the 1890s:

> The whole generation is womanized; the masculine tone is passing out of the world; it's a feminine, a nervous, hysterical, chattering, canting age, an age of hollow phrases, and false delicacy and exaggerated solicitudes and coddled sensibilities, which, if we don't soon look out, will usher in the reign of mediocrity, of the feeblest and flattest and the most pretentious that has ever been. (James, 2013: 334)

This statement comes from Henry James's dubious hero Basil Ransom in *The Bostonians* and his statement is not an exceptional opinion. As a matter of fact, Ransom's attack on what he perceives to be an inferior and feminized culture at the fin de siècle was echoed by many contemporary cultural commentators (Ledger, 1997: 177). In other words, high-quality writing is, in general, in these commentators' opinion, supposed to be masculine and impersonal. In view of the anxieties about the feminization of American culture at the fin de siècle as well as the denigration of feminine writing as nervous, hysterical, hollow, false, exaggerated, mediocre, feeble, flat, pretentious and so on, it is not at all surprising that Cather would do her best to keep a far distance from those female writers.

The trajectory of Cather's evolving attitude toward domestic activities can be perceived from the ways she delineates foodways throughout her literary career. Domesticity and the kingdom of art are mutually exclusive in Cather's early short stories, such as "A Wagner Matinée" and "The Garden Lodge". In "A Wagner Matinée" narrated from the perspective of a young man named Clark, Cather demonstrates how the sheer routine and harsh labor of everyday life such as cooking and washing-up are enemies to the development of one's musical talent. For Clark, much of Aunt Georgianna's talent in Latin grammar, Greek mythology, Shakespeare and music is "dissolved in soapsuds, or worked into bread, or milked into the bottom of a pail" (*EN* 109).① In the second story, the heroine, Caroline Noble, recalls that in her childhood, while her house was a place where a "mystic worship of things distant, intangible and unattainable" prevailed, the family nevertheless always had "to come down to the cold facts of the case; to boiled mutton and to the necessity of turning the dining-room carpet" (*EN* 51).

In her first novel *Alexander's Bridge*, Cather does not attach great importance to food and cooking. In "My First Novel", Cather compares *Alexander's Bridge* to what painters call a studio picture. In the words of Cather, this novel is set more or less in London and it follows the most conventional pattern of novels of her day. Alexander eats and drinks champagne in Hilda's place, they have lunch at Richmond, and they dine in a little French place in Soho. There is sometimes detailed description about what the characters eat, drink and the atmosphere of the place where they dine together as well. For instance, Alexander's dinner in Hilda's place was a wonderful little dinner. There was watercress soup, a delightful omelette stuffed with mushrooms and truffles, two small rare ducklings and artichokes, and a dry yellow Rhone wine of which Bartley had always been very fond. This type of dinner looks dazzling yet it lacks warmth and depth of meaning emanating from the description of food in her later works.

In *O Pioneers!*, Mrs. Bergson emerges as the first good housewife that Cather highly celebrates in her major works. Mrs. Bergson loves comfort and for eleven years after they settle down, "she had worthily striven to maintain some semblance of household order amid conditions that made order very difficult". (*OP* 151) Mrs. Bergson's way of keeping "the family from disintegrating morally and getting careless in their ways" is to "repeat the routine of her old life among new surroundings"(*OP* 151). Mrs. Bergson insists on her own way of housekeeping not only to establish a sense of belonging in the new environment, but also to

---

① When the story is published, the similarities shared between Aunt Georgianna and Cather's aunt offend Cather's relatives and make them rather unhappy. When the story is recollected fifteen years later in *Youth and the Bright Medusa*, Cather softens her description of the harshness of Aunt Georgianna's pioneering life, and the part I cite is actually deleted in the 1920 version.

distinguish her style from her slovenly neighbors.① She misses the fish diet of her own country so much that "twice every summer she sent the boys to the river, twenty miles to the southward, to fish for channel cat. When the children were little she used to load them all into the wagon, the baby in its crib, and go fishing herself" (*OP* 151-152). Mrs. Bergson is obsessed with "preserving" and "stout as she was, she roamed the scrubby banks of Norway Creek looking for fox grapes and goose plums, like a wild creature in search of prey" (*OP* 152). Confronted with the scarcity of food of the new circumstance, she gives full play to her intelligence and imagination. "She made a yellow jam of the insipid ground-cherries that grew on the prairie, flavoring it with lemon peel; and she made a sticky dark conserve of garden tomatoes. She had experimented even with the rank buffalo-pea." (*OP* 152) It is for the determination and intelligence displayed by housewives like Mrs. Bergson that Cather remarks,

> The farmer wife who raises a large family and cooks for them and makes their clothes and keeps house and on the side runs a truck garden and a chicken farm and a canning establishment, and thoroughly enjoys doing it all, and doing it well, contributes more to art than all the culture clubs. Often you find such a woman with all the appreciation of the beautiful bodies of her children, of the order and harmony of her kitchen, of the real creative joy of all her activities, which marks the great artist. (*WCP* 47)

In the novels following the publication of *O Pioneers!*, such as *The Song of the Lark*, *My Ántonia* and *One of Ours*, again and again, Cather creates a number of female characters like Mrs. Lorch, Mrs. Burdens, Mrs. Harling, Ántonia and Old Mahailey. These women are plain ordinary housewives, yet through the capability and passion they manifest for their work, they manage to subvert the stereotypical ideas about

---

① Cather hates slovenliness and dirtiness. In *A Lost Lady*, a novella she publishes ten years after *O Pioneers!*, from the perspective of her narrator, Niel, Cather articulates her disapproval of a slovenly living style. In the novel, Niel's childhood home is kept by a poor cousin from Kentucky who always leaves washing lying about in various stages of completion. For her lousiness, Niel concludes, she is probably the worst housekeeper in the world.

doing-cooking and hence give significance to their work. Like great artists, Cather's capable cooks nourish not only the bodies of her characters but also their souls. Cather herself recalled fondly of the inspiration she had drawn from her time with these capable housewives. "I have never found any intellectual excitement, any more intense than I used to feel when I spent a morning with one of those old women at her baking or butter making. I used to ride home in the most unreasonable state of excitement." (*WCP* 10)

Mrs. Lorch, Thea's landlady in Chicago, is an excellent cook. Thea confesses that she has never been so well nourished before (*EN* 442). In Cather's fiction, the act of feeding the body (especially the body of the artist) has "sanctity" that can even "attain to an artistic status of its own" (Meyering, 1994: 104). Doing-cooking is never dreary for Mrs. Harling of *My Ántonia*, and in her household, "preserving-time was a prolonged festival" (*EN* 807). The joyful atmosphere in Mrs. Harling's kitchen exerts considerable influence on Ántonia, who says she will "never have known anything about cooking or housekeeping"(*EN* 921) if she does not spend some time with Mrs. Harling.

Old Mahailey, the housekeeper of the Wheeler's in *One of Ours* is modeled on Cather's servant Marjorie ("Margie") Anderson, who came to Nebraska with Charles Cather's family from Back Creek, Virginia, in 1883. Like Mary in "Neighbor Rosicky", Mahailey "liked to see the men fill themselves with food" (*LN* 95). Due to the impact of the memory of hunger in her youth, Mahailey's philosophy of food can be to some extent narrow-minded, as when she lies to save pickled peaches for her favorite boy (*LN* 75), yet it could be equally all-embracing. With no knowledge other than that concerned with cooking, Mahailey figures out everything about World War I in terms of cooking and food. Unfamiliar with gas-masks worn by the soldiers of World War I, Mahailey "worked it out for herself that these masks were worn by the army cooks, to protect their eyes when they were cutting up onions! 'All them onions they have to cut up, it could put their eyes out if they didn't wear somethin', she argued" (*LN* 232). Statements such as these sound laughable, yet there is no denying true wisdom in what Mahailey senses the imminent doom brought by World War I as embodied in the poor old lady she sees in the Red Cross poster, "Where's she goin' to, anyways? See, Mr. Claude, she's got her iron cook-pot, pore old thing, carryin' it all the way!" (*LN* 233)

Characters such as Mrs. Lorch, Mrs. Burdens, Mrs. Harling, Ántonia and Old Mahailey are categorized by Bearrie Laura Lyn Pogue as the "traditional feeders" in Cather's fiction. Cather's "traditional feeders" bear a close resemblance to the heroines of the fiction of the nineteenth-century sentimentalists, yet without their sentimentality. For instance, none of Cather's female "traditional feeders" give the impression of being "the angel of the house". Instead, most of them are tough immigrant housewives who work hard to maintain the survival of their family in an alien world. In addition to these "traditional feeders" in her fiction, Cather also creates another group of female characters (such as Alexandra in *O Pioneers!* and Thea in *The Song of the Lark*), who resolved to liberate themselves from the kitchen and male figures who are quite devoted to cooking (such as Peter of *My Ántonia* and the two bishops in *Death Comes for the Archbishop*), thus subverting traditional concepts on the relationship between gender and cooking.

Unlike her mother Mrs. Bergson, Alexandra in *O Pioneers!* is seldom engaged with cooking by herself. Rather, Alexandra has the housework done by three pretty young Swedish girls, who "cook and pickle and preserve all summer long" (*OP* 51) in her kitchen. Leaving behind the chores of the interior space, Alexandra expresses herself best in the soil (*OP* 178). By placing her female character in a setting totally different from that of her predecessors', Cather creates a new heroine in American literature (O'Brien, 1982: 280). The image of Alexandra as an pioneer and farm manager is quite revolutionary for it not only contradicts Frederick Jackson Turner's envisioning of the frontier hero as a male (Dyck, 2013: 163), but also subverts the traditional assumption of a woman's place in the house. For the arrangement of the seats at the table during dinner often shows the distribution of power among all the eaters, Alexandra always seated at the head of the long table.

Alexandra is a born entrepreneur. Her father knew it, and that's why he entrusted the future of the whole family to his daughter rather than his sons on his deathbed. Alexandra manifests great foresight when she insists on buying more land at the critical moment. The Bergsons prospered after Alexandra took over as the head of the house. And they became the owner of one of the richest farms on the Divide. By taking control of the land, Alexandra becomes a provider in a real sense of the word. In the novel, Cather states clearly that the land is the food. During the harvest season, "everywhere the grain stood ripe and the hot afternoon was full of the smell of the ripe wheat, like the smell of bread baking in an oven". (*OP* 158)

In *O Pioneers!*, Cather creates not only a new heroine in American literature, who is unprecedentedly "strong, autonomous, creative" (O'Brien, 1982: 280), but also a new kind of relationship between human beings and the land. E. K. Brown and Leon Edel maintain that "at the heart of her feeling for the land is a poetic appreciation that no character preceded her in Willa Cather's fiction had even adumbrated" (1953:176). O'Brien claims that Alexandra's "passion for the land" makes her "the novel's supreme artist" (1982: 280). Similarily, Brown and Edel conclude that the pioneer and the artist are generally the same figure in Cather's fiction, for "underneath all the distinctions that separated them, and more telling than any, was the impulse they shared to turn from their own tracks of routine and convention to make a track of their own"(1953: x). In this way, Alexandra bears a striking resemblance to the group of cooking "artists" (such as Mrs. Bergson, Old Mahailey) that I have discussed in the earlier part of this chapter. Alexandra displays as much passion and inventiveness for the land as the cooking "artists" for their dishes. In *O Pioneers!*, even though Alexandra is not directly involved in the activity of cooking, her work still has much to do with food itself. In addition, her intimate relationship with those who are good at cooking and baking, such as the three Swedish girls and Marie, makes it easier for her to assimilate herself into the community of cooking women.

When Cather made the heroine of *The Song of the Lark* an artist, she was not making an unusual choice. In a fiction by women at the fin de siècle, the figure of the woman artist appears almost obsessively (Ammons, 1992: 121). Different from Alexandra, Thea's profession has nothing to do with food. Nevertheless, food plays an important role in both her personal and professional life. In *The Song of the Lark*, Cather often uses Thea's physical response to food as a metaphor to symbolize her artistic development. For instance, even when she was a little girl, Thea was sensitive to the beauty and texture of Malaga grapes that Dr. Archie gave to her. Here is Thea's response to the grapes, "she was holding the almost transparent fruit up in the sunlight, feeling the pale-green skins softly with the tips of her fingers". (*EN* 304) Dr. Archie gives Thea grapes instead of other fruit because grapes are the very fruit which suggests "the accumulated knowledge of Western civilization" (Leder, 1997: 57) in both biblical and classical traditions.

Living in a mediocre boarding-house as a music student in Chicago, Thea was given "poor food for body and mind" (*EN* 470). Each time she moved into a new place, her eyes challenged the food of the house (*EN* 518). Thea's fastidiousness about food is shared by other artists or people with artistic inclinations in the novel. Mr. Larsen, the preacher who also "managed the music in his church himself and drilled his choir was fussy about his food" (*EN* 438); "good food, good cigars, a little good wine" (*EN* 455) meant a great deal to Thea's teacher Mr. Harsanyi; Theodore Thomas, the conductor, complained of bad food on his tour; Bowers (one of Thea's teachers) liked good food (*EN* 528); and Thea's patron Frederick "knew as much about food and wines as any man in Chicago" (*EN* 527).

Also those fragments of pottery that Thea found during her stay at Panther Canyon impelled her to have an epiphany about art:

> This care, expended upon vessels that could not hold food or water any better for the additional labor put upon them, made her heart go out to those ancient potters. They had not only expressed their desire, but they had experienced it as beautifully as they could. Food, fire, water, and something else—even here, in this crack in the world, so far back in the night of the past! Down here at the beginning that painful thing was already stirring; the seed of sorrow, and of so much delight. (*EN* 553)

By the time she has become a famous singer, Thea reveals to Dr. Archie her gratefulness to Frederick during her apprenticeship years and she defines the kind of help Frederick offered to her in terms of food. "Frederick is still feeding me. I would have died of starvation at that boarding-house on Indiana Avenue if he hadn't taken me out to the Buckingham and filled me up once in a while. What a cavern I was to fill, too. The waiters used to look astonished. I'm still singing on that food." (*EN* 665) Just as Cather's food is full of rich meanings, hunger in Cather's works can be understood in different ways (Shively, 2010: 81). Thea's hunger for food should be understood both physically and mentally. Mentally, Thea's hunger for food represents her yearning to break through and to achieve artistic success.

Not all female characters that make up their minds to disengage themselves from housekeeping are highly celebrated in Cather's works; others are severely criticized. Enid Royce in *One of Ours* is a typical case in point. Enid has judgment that is just as good as Frances Harling[①] in *My Ántonia* or Tommy[②] in "Tommy the Unsentimental". Mr. Royce says that if Enid were to be taken into his office, she might run a business better than a house. Given the intelligence, courage and determination she displays, Enid might have proved herself to be as capable as Cather's earlier pioneers, such as Alexandra and Tiny Sodderball[③]. Yet the God of Destiny decides otherwise. Enid is not at all a "nest-building bird", but she was, nevertheless, dragged into marriage—with disastrous results.

Along with Mrs. Archie from *The Song of the Lark*, Enid becomes another of Cather's notorious housewife. Mrs. Archie is only a minor character in *The Song of the Lark*, yet she sets the precedent for Cather's notorious housewives. Her disinterest in food and cooking may be of a different kind than that of Enid's, yet Cather's description of Mrs. Archie, to some degree, foreshadows the character of Enid in *One of Ours*. Both women fail to nourish their husband in body and soul, and neither of

---

[①] Frances Harling is a girl with unusual business ability. She is her father's chief clerk, and virtually manages his Black Hawk office during his frequent absences.

[②] For Tommy, Cather presents a female protagonist who would flout conventional gender role and sexual designation in nearly every aspect of her life. Her appearance is decidedly unfeminine. Tommy plays whist and billiards, drinks cocktails, earns the respect of her father's business friends. Tommy rides a bicycle, which, Patricia Marks has observed, is one of the signatures of New Woman activities.

[③] Of all the girls and boys who grow up together in Black Hawk, Tiny Sodderball becomes a shrewd manager in the economic world and she leads the most adventurous life and achieves the most solid worldly success.

them bear their husband a child. "Mrs. Archie felt no interest in food herself, and she hated to prepare it. She liked nothing better than to have Dr. Archie go Denver for a few days... and to be left alone to eat canned salmon and to keep the house shut up from morning until night." (*EN* 322)

Enid practices prohibition on humankind, on the hens, and she leaves her husband "eating a cold supper by himself" (*OO* 204). Cather's former new women figures such as Alexandra, Ántonia and Thea are also defiant of traditional gender roles, yet none of them seem to be as loathsome as Enid. What sets Enid apart from other new women figures in Cather's works is her threatening modernity, which has much to do with the turbulent background of wartime America. Enid's vegetarianism①, together with her scientific farming②, comes directly from publicity disseminated during the wartime, in which "Eat Less Meat" and "Eat Less Wheat" were popular demands (James, 2013: 50). For her husband's supper, Enid arranges "a dish of canned salmon with a white sauce; hardboiled eggs, peeled and lying in a nest of lettuce leaves; a bowl of ripe tomatoes, a bit of cold rice pudding; cream and butter" (*OO* 201). Enid's supper reflects the influence of the new science of home economics that Warren Belasco and Harvey Levenstein term as "the New Nutrition", a Progressive Era paradigm that defines cooking as a scientific activity through which women could achieve an ideal balance of the properties of different food groups. Enid's supper may provide nourishment yet it is never what "a man could look forward to with pleasure or sit down to with satisfaction" (*OO* 122).

Enid, Alexandra, Tommy, Tiny, Lena and Thea all belong to the category of new women figures in Cather's fiction. Similarities shared by this group of new women figures are that they are hard-working, strong, tough and more importantly, they seem

---

① Even before her marriage, Enid practices vegetarianism with her mother. Additionally every summer Mrs. Royce goes to a vegetarian sanatorium in Michigan, where she learns to live on nuts and toasted cereals.

② During the wartime, U.S. Food Administration distributed a series of posters with a purpose to indoctrinate a primarily female audience into a new science of domestic economy. And one poster in this series informs its readers that unfertilized poultry eggs "last longer"—a piece of scientific information that Enid puts to use by keeping her hens separate from the rooster.

to attach more importance to their career than to their personal life—be it romantic love or marriage. As a literary phenomenon, the New Woman seems to have more affiliations with British literature than with American literature. The term itself first appeared in Sarah Grand's 1894 essay "The New Aspect of the Woman Question", in which she claimed that "the new woman... has been sitting apart in silent contemplation all these years... until at last she solved the problem and proclaimed for herself what was wrong with Home-is-the-Woman's Sphere, and prescribed the remedy" (Molino, 2011: 98). Almost all the books concerning this topic are about British literature, such as Lloyd Fernando's *"New Women" in the Late Victorian Novel*, Gail Cunningham's *The New Woman and the Victorian Novel*, Ann Aridis's *New Women, New Novels: Feminism and Early Modernism* and Teresa Mangum's *Married, Middlebrow, and Militant: Sarah Grand and the New Woman Novel*. All these monographs interpret New Woman as a particular British literary phenomenon, with British women writers like Sarah Grand, Mona Carid, Lucas Malet, Ella Hepworth Dixon and Mary Cholmondeley as the representative new women writers.

Yet the New Woman as a powerful social-literary phenomenon did exist in American literature by the late nineteenth century. Moreover, as an embodiment of new values, the New Woman posed a critical challenge to the existing social order and exerted great influence on the national literature. "From the 1890s the new woman—independent, outspoken, iconoclastic—empowered the work of Kate Chopin, Alice James, Charlotte Perkins Gilman, Edith Wharton, Ellen Glasgow, Willa Cather, and the young Gertrude Stein." (Elliot, 1988: 589) New Woman fiction such as Sarah Orne Jewett's *A Country Doctor* and Kate Chopin's *The Awakening* challenged the received wisdom on courtship, marriage and the family, rejecting such truths as the maternal instinct and the role of child-rearing as the highest duty of women (Elliot,1998: 590).

Among all of Cather's works, there is not a single novel that contains so many new women images as there are in *My Ántonia*. The behavior of hired girls in *My Ántonia*, for instance, overthrows the Victorian image of women as the domestic angels in the house. After her father's death, Ántonia takes it as her responsibility to "make this land one good farm" (*EN* 792) and when spring comes, she goes with her brother into the fields and plows like a man; Ántonia once tells Jim that she would "better like to work out-of-doors than in a house" (*EN* 801) and does not care if it makes her like a man.

Cather's hired girls inhabit a wilder sphere, which enables them to push their energies to the greatest extent. The lifestyle of Cather's professional women characters like Lena Lingard and Tiny Soderball offers new possibilities beyond the backbreaking labors of prairie farming or passionless marriage life. Lena is determined not to be trapped by the bondage of marriage life, because she doesn't want to stick at home all the time and be accountable to anybody (*EN* 892). This decision to live a single life is significant because the capability of making a conscious choice itself is "a hallmark of the identity of the new woman" (Elliot, 1988: 592).

Yet behind these celebrations, through the perspective of the narrator, Jim, Cather shows that she is quite aware of the hostility these working girls may incur from the society — "the country girls were considered (by the town people) a menace to the social order. Their beauty shone out too boldly against a conventional background" (*EN* 840). By the end of the story, while Ántonia is the only hired girl who lives her life to the fullest by becoming a mother of fourteen children, Tiny Soderball, in contrast, becomes a "thin, hard-faced" woman and her "faculty of becoming interested is worn out" (*EN* 896-897).

The sharp contrast between Ántonia's and Tiny's lives (Cather's celebration of new women figures like Alexander and Thea juxtaposed with her condemnation of new women figures like Enid) seems to indicate Cather's ambivalent attitude toward both the new women figures and her female literary heritage. In turning her attention to new women figures who walk out of their homes and devote themselves to the development of their careers, Cather may seem to liberate herself from the entrapment of the traditional domestic plot. Yet, she is not that far away from her female literary predecessors; home plot and domestic ritual still occupy a significant place in Cather's fiction. Cather's new women figures may have more options when compared to their Victorian sisters. Nevertheless, more often than not, domesticity still serves as an important background against which these new women figures are measured. It is these new women figures who can handle both their domestic duties and their professional lives well that seem to win the favor of the author. This metric explains why, of all the new women figures in *My Ántonia*, Cather only singles Ántonia out for praise.

In addition to developing female characters who challenge her contemporary readers' traditional expectations of femininity, Cather also creates a number of male characters who are keen on cooking and successfully adopt the role that used to be adopted by traditional housewives. Characters of this kind include Peter in *My Ántonia*, who is fond of his cow and could "make butter by beating sour cream with a wooden spoon" (*EN* 734); the two bishops in *Death Comes for the Archbishop*, with Father Joseph quite good at cooking and Bishop Latour meticulous about his garden; and Old Henry in *The Professor's House*, who is a wonderful cook and a good housekeeper (*LN* 218). Cather's creation of "feminized" men figures is one of the main reasons for the wide controversy over her sexuality. Yet I want to argue that like her creation of new women figures in her fiction, Cather's portrayal of the abovementioned men figures is a strategy to provide new alternatives to the traditional domestic plot. Cather uses the discourse of feeding and eating to interrogate and extend the traditional female role model and to break the stereotypical association between gender and cooking.

In truth, Cather is not alone of course among fin de siècle female writers who are preoccupied with food writing of various kinds. For instance, Bearrie Laura Lyn Pogue's dissertation "Devouring Words", shows both Kate Chopin's and Edith Wharton's concern with eating and feeding in some of their works. As for the reasons why writers are so fascinated by the discourse of food, Samuel J. Rogal comments,

> Perhaps the general and collective attraction to food and drink for literati (or artists of other forms and genres) stems from the realization that items heaped upon plates or poured into goblet allow the sharp, imaginative eye of the poet or prose writer to focus upon the most basic instincts: on one hand, the need to sustain life, on the other to escape from it. No matter how intense the drama or trauma of life, no matter how passionate the ecstasy or how intense the hatred, no matter how desperate the frustration or how

wonderful the achievement, at certain (and usually regular) moments during the physical or spiritual flow of human activity, persons must pause to eat and to drink. (1997: 3)

So it is in the sense that food and drink point to the basic instincts of human beings that both writers and readers alike are drawn to the discourse of food. Food is at once primordial and instrumental and one's nostalgic imagination is quite often steeped in the sentimental sense-memory of food (Cozzi, 2010: 11). The smell of gingerbread baking from his grandma's kitchen lingers in Jim's memory even after many years. The importance of the activity of food-eating is demonstrated by Jim's declaration in the novel *My Ántonia* that "our lives centered on warmth and food" (*EN* 754).

## 3.2 The Smells of the Past in "Neighbor Rosicky" and *My Ántonia*

In the words of Giard, doing-cooking is never simply the more or less inventive response to the limitations of circumstance; it always smells and tastes of the past (qtd. in de Certeau et al., 1998: 152). Food memories figure as a central element for Cather's immigrants' recreation of everyday life in a new country. Mrs. Bergson's nostalgia for the fish diet of her own country is shared by Cather's other immigrants. In *My Ántonia*, after weeks of life on the ocean, the Shimerdas are famished for fruit. The two daughters would wander for miles along the edge of the cornfields, hunting for ground-cherries (*EN* 731). Peter, a Russian, gorges himself on watermelons and winter melons because they remind him of the village of his childhood, where melons are considered "better than medicine" (*EN* 735). Anna, one of the hired girls, says that her grandmother keeps asking her mother to take her down to the waterside and the fish market: "She craves fish all the time. Whenever I go home I take her canned salmon and mackerel" (*EN* 862). One of the most significant reasons for Cather's immigrants' yearning for the food of the familiar taste of their homeland is that for them, "food acts as a veritable discourse of the past and a nostalgic narrative about the country, the region, the city, or the village where one was born" (qtd. in de Certeau et al., 1998: 184). To obtain once again the food one used to have access to in the new land helps to alleviate the pain caused by immigration and to establish a sense of belonging. In Peter's case, the juicy fruit is metaphorically a medicine that could palliate his homesickness. Similarly, Tiny Soderball tells her friends that it seems that her mother has not been so homesick since her father began growing rye flour for her (*EN* 862).

The imprints of food on the past evoke both pleasant and sad memories. It is often the case that it is hard to find clear-cut distinctions between the sweetness and the bitterness of life. Among all of the short stories (there are more than sixty) written by Cather during her career, "Neighbor Rosicky" is considered one of her most memorable (Arnold, 1984: 135). The story also marks an important turning point in her writing career. In "Neighbor Rosicky", Cather returns for the first time to a Nebraska setting she knew in her youth, which she explored in "The Bohemian Girl". The story is about the last year of Rosicky's life. More precisely, it is about Rosicky's remembrance of and reflection upon his life. This story triumphs as "a celebration of old-fashioned American agrarian values—immigrant hopefulness in the land of opportunity, self-help, honesty, pleasure in the everyday, domestic order, endurance" (Lee, 1989: 310).

"Neighbor Rosicky" is filled with food descriptions. Rosicky's warm kitchen is also full of the smell of coffee and hot biscuit and sausage (*SPW* 589). In "Neighbor Rosicky", food is presented as having more significance than something that simply sustains life: it is also a reward for labor, a connection to the Rosicky's Czech past, and the medium for establishing emotional bonds with family, friends and animals (Danker, 1990: 24-28). For Mary, Rosicky's wife, to feed creatures was the natural expression of affection—her chickens, the calves, her big hungry boys. Also she finds much pleasure in providing food to a young man like Doctor Burleigh[①], whom she seldom sees and of whom she is as proud as if he belongs to her (*SPW* 590). "Neighbor Rosicky" is about the story of Rosicky's past experience, yet Rosicky does not yearn for the past when he had known loneliness and hunger and poverty; rather, he sets them against the present and is grateful (Arnold, 1984: 136).

In "Neighbor Rosicky", Cather's skeptical attitude towards modernity and her

---

[①] Doctor Burleigh or Doctor Ed. has known Rosicky almost ever since he could remember. In the story, Dr. Burleigh is one narrator who from time to time gives comments on the Rosickys, yet Dr. Burleigh never threatens to become the focus of the story as Jim Burden in *My Ántonia* does.

preoccupation with nineteenth-century agrarian culture is made all too obvious in her arrangement of the sharp contrast between Rosicky's later living experience in the countryside and his earlier life in two cities—New York and London. Two events from the past exert considerable influence on Rosicky's perception of life. The first event has much to do with the hard times Rosicky went through in London when he was a young man. It was Christmas time, and "all de windows is full of good t'ings to eat, an' all de pushcarts in de streets is full" (*SPW* 609).[①] Yet Rosicky had no money. In order to give her family and all the tenants a good dinner on Christmas Day, Mrs. Lifschnitz, the landlady, gave the tenants nothing but a little bread dripping the day before Christmas. During the night, Rosicky was hungry and worse still, the moment he put his head down to sleep, he smelt something good. The smell got stronger and stronger and it made Rosicky sleepless. The good smell is the smell of a roast goose that the landlady hid in the box. Ultimately, young Rosicky fails to resist the temptation to have only one little bite of that goose; instead, he eats half of that.

In the end, Rosicky is lucky enough to meet some generous town people who helped him make up for the mistake he had made, but the experience of this whole event lingers in Rosicky's mind and exerts great influence on the Rosicky's attitude toward life. Mary says she would rather put some color into her children's faces than put money into the bank (*SPW* 597). Doctor Ed. reflects, "Maybe… people as generous and warmhearted, and affectionate as the Rosickys never got ahead much; maybe you couldn't enjoy your life and put it in the bank, too." (*SPW* 592)

Rosicky's philosophy of life, according to which physical and spiritual wellbeing rather than monetary gain is the first and foremost important thing in one's life, is also reflected in another event. This time, the story is told by his wife, Mary. It happened on one Fourth of July when there was terrible hot wind, which burned everything up. The neighbors were discouraged, and "some of 'em grieved till they got poor digestions" (*SPW* 608). Poor as the Rosickys were, they managed to relish what they did have. Their dinner could not have been more sumptuous for supper: they had a bottle of wildgrape wine, fried chicken, and plums on hot biscuit, and they

---

① Rosicky is of Czech origin; hence he has some difficulty in telling a long story in English.

ate their supper behind the mulberry hedge, under the linden trees (*SPW* 607).

In "Neighbor Rosicky", Cather uses food as a recurrent motif throughout the whole story. When he talks about his past to his children, Rosicky admits that he always "had a good appetite" (*SPW* 609). This appetite has as much to do with both Rosicky's desire for food as it does with his philosophy of life—to live life to the fullest even in face of adversity. From his past, Rosicky learned the bitterness of hunger and starvation; nevertheless, he also harvests an understanding of the right kind of life he could possibly pursue.

There is another way to understand the past of Giard's "doing cooking, always smells and tastes of the past" (qtd. in de Certeau et al., 1998: 152). This past could signify both memories linked to past experience and reasons for the existence of mistrust—the prejudices against the other's culinary customs. We do our own style of cooking, our cuisine, the way we used to do over there, so as to make distinction between the alimentary time of the self and the alimentary time of the other (*SPW* 184). In *Shadows on the Rock*, Madame Auclair is proud of her French origin: "we are conscientious, and that is why we are called the most civilized people in Europe and other nations envy us" (*LN* 479). Before her death, she tries her best to inculcate the sense of "our way" in her daughter's mind. In the opinion of Madame Auclair, careless people got through the winter on smoked eels and frozen fish, "conscientious" people on the other hand could live very well, even in Quebec (*SPW* 493).

In *My Ántonia*, when the Burdens pay visit to the Shimerdas, Jim says that they are horrified to see the "sour, ashy-gray bread" that Mrs. Shimerda gives her family to eat. Then Jim details the way as to how Mrs. Shimerda makes yeast so as to give an example to show the primitiveness of Mrs. Shimerda's cooking method. "When she took the paste out to bake it, she left smears of dough sticking to the sides of the measure, put the measure on the shelf behind the stove, and let this residue ferment. The next time, she made bread, she scraped this sour stuff down into the fresh dough to serve as yeast." (*NS* 732) On another occasion, to repay the Burdens for their kindness and generosity, Mrs. Shimerda gives a teacup of mushrooms to Jim's grandmother. To manifest the culinary prejudice the Shimerdas and the Burdens hold against each other, Cather details the reaction of all the people around. At the sight of the bag of the mushrooms, Ántonia's crazy brother "began to smack his lips" (*NS* 762). Clearly, what is contained in the bag reminds him of something delicious. Cather then foregrounds Jim's sensual impression of the stuff: "it gave out a salty, earthy smell, very pungent, even among the other odors of that cave"(*NS* 762). Jim's strong sense of repugnance towards what Mrs. Shimerda is going to give him forms a sharp contrast with Mrs. Shimerda's ceremonious presentation of the gift:

> Mrs. Shimerda measured a teacup full, tied it up in a bit of sacking, and presented it ceremoniously to grandmother.
> "For cook," she announced. "Little now; be very much when cook," spreading out her hands as if to indicate that the pint would swell to a gallon. "Very good. You no have in this country. All things for eat better in my country." (*NS* 762)

As to Mrs. Shimerda's boast, Grandma Burden responds drily, "maybe so, Mrs. Shimerda—I can't say but I prefer our bread to yours, myself." To lighten the atmosphere of the conversation between her mother and Mrs. Shimerda, Ántonia also joins the conversation, trying her best to convince Mrs. Burden of the goodness of their mushrooms. "This is very good, Mrs. Burden—she clasped her hands as if she could not express how good… 'Oh, so good!'" (*NS* 763) Yet, in the end, neither Mrs. Shimerda nor Ántonia succeeds in persuading the Burdens of the superiority of their food. Mrs. Burden in particular adopts a dubious attitude towards the gift that Mrs. Shimerda has given to her. That night, after they go back home, the Burdens still regard the gift both Mrs. Shimerda and Ántonia highly value as something weird, strange or even dangerous. "We could not determine whether they were animal or vegetable. They might be dried meat from some queer beast, Jim. They ain't dried fish, and they never grew on stalk or vine. I'm afraid of 'em'." (*NS* 763) Eventually, the package is thrown into the stove and burned into ashes.

The reasons for the wide gap between the Shimerdas' and the Burdens' perception of food and the deep mistrust and prejudice they hold against each other may have something to do with their different social and racial status. The Burdens are of higher social status than the Shimerdas, thus Mrs. Burden considers her way of cooking and eating superior to that of the Shimerdas'. The Burdens are a local family whereas the Shimerdas are immigrants. This scene is evidence of how a lack of the cultural communication among different ethnic groups can lead to mistrust of and disrespect for the other's culture.

The Shimerdas, of course, are not the only family whose way of cooking and eating is questioned by the locals. Jim says he has never seen anyone eat so many watermelons as the Russian Peter eats. Even though Peter assures him that "they were good for one—better than medicine; in his own country people lived on them at the time of year" (*NS* 735). Once when Jim and Ántonia came back home from their visit to the two Russians, Peter gave ripe cucumbers and a lard-pail full of milk for Mrs. Shimerda to cook, to which Jim reflected that he had never heard of cooking cucumbers (*NS* 735). Even though Cather does not mention the outcome of these cucumbers, readers have reason to believe that they may end as badly as the mushrooms. Cather claims that "the Americanization committee worker who persuades an old Bohemian housewife that it is better for her to feed her family out of tin cans instead of cooking them a steaming goose for dinner is committing a crime against art" (*WCP* 147). Through bringing diverse ethnic food into dialogue in *My Ántonia*, Cather attempts to make a strong argument for the central role of quality food in the establishment of a diverse but harmonious and satisfyingly complex American life (Jewell, 2010: 72).

## 3.3 The Cultural Aspect of Cather's Foodways

In Cather's works, the rich meaning of her foodways is reflected not only on the part of the cooks, but also on the side of the eaters. Giles claims that "preparing and cooking fresh foods was a signifier of a certain 'cultural capital' " (2004: 116). Barthes also demonstrates that the cultural messages encoded by the acts of eating depend not only on their substances or their contents, but also on their techniques of preparation and habits of consumption, or their context—how, why, when, where, and by whom the units of signification are prepared and eaten (1961: 22). In the case of Cather's writings, I want to argue that the "what, where, when, with whom and how" one eats is often used by the author to indicate the social identity of the eaters and to measure the stability of the world. At the beginning of *My Ántonia,* what sets the Shimerdas apart from the Burdens is the food they eat. While the Shimerdas live on "corncakes and sorghum molasses" and "sour, ashy-gray bread" (*NS* 727-732), the Burdens can afford as much chicken as they can eat on Sundays, and on other days, they have plenty of "ham or bacon or sausages meat" (*NS* 754).

Similarly, in *Shadows on the Rock*, the small town of Quebec is stratified by class as much as by the discourse of food. The Auclairs have a relationship of mutual dependence with the elites of the town, hence they could afford to make conserves while their poor neighbors could not (*LN* 471). Whereas grease is meat to most of the neighborhood of Quebec, the Auclairs could have large amount of lard at their disposal (*LN* 494). Morning begins at the Auclairs' with a pot of chocolate (*LN* 474). Cécile's little protégé Jacques notices that the Auclairs is the only house in the world he knows in which that comforting drink "chocolate" is made (*LN* 519). Cather's inclusion of chocolate in the novel is deeply nuanced, particularly if one takes into account the role of chocolate in the history of Europe and the Americas (Jewell, 2010: 284). In 1697, the year in which Cather's story begins, chocolate had been in France—and, by extension, its colony in Canada—for only a few decades. Therefore, the presence of chocolate in the Auclair home as well as in the Bishop Laval's testifies to the privileged status of its consumers.

In *Shadows on the Rock*, the Auclairs' distinguished social place in the whole community is conveyed not only through the kind of food and drink they could have access to, but also through the way in which food is prepared and consumed in their household. Of the three meals, dinner is "the important event of the day" and Mr. Auclair regards his dinner the very thing that "kept him a civilized man and a Frenchman" (*LN* 474). While the savage may live on eating "the flesh of dogs" and "corn-meal boiled in dirty water and dirty kettles"(*LN* 560) and the uncivilized cook everything in grease, the Auclairs dine with due form. The apothecary and his daughter dine at the fixed time, six o'clock in winter and seven in summer; they begin with the soup, the main dishes and the wine; after that, they have several options for their dessert (*LN* 469-471). The Auclairs' meticulous attention to every detail of their dinner (time, order of dishes) indicates that dinner in the Auclairs' home is never plain eating. The Auclairs' daily consumption of food and drink as well as those instruments laid on the dinner table—Cécile set their dining-table with "a white cloth, silver candlesticks, glasses, and two clear decanters, one of red wine and one of white" (*LN* 469)—becomes an index of the kind of life the Auclairs live. It signifies order, stability and security in the household of the Auclairs.

What Cécile and her father could enjoy during peaceful times forms a sharp contrast with what they could maintain during the time of crisis. When Mr. Auclair's patron, the count is dying, Mr. Auclair neglects his common duties of "putting away any wood-dove in fat, or laid in winter vegetables, or bought his supply of wild rice from the Indians" (*LN* 623). When Pierre comes to visit, Cécile feels deeply mortified to confess that they have not much to offer to their dear friend (*LN* 632). What the Auclairs have for their dinner table is of course not as destitute as Cécile claims—they still have "some wild rice left from last year, some carrots, preserves, soup and a bottle of heavy gold-colored wine from the South" (*LN* 632). Yet it is definitely destitute in comparison with the dishes Cécile could have given in the good old days. When Father Hector comes for dinner at the Auclairs', Cécile gives him "fish soup with which she have taken such pains, and the wood doves, cooked in a casserole with mushrooms and served with wild rice" (*LN* 557-558). The contrast between the two dinner scenes indicates the instability of the world and the altering of the social order. The disorder Cécile experiences in their dinner table is also a reflection of the inner insecurity and the lack of reassurance both she and her father feel when their world falls into crisis. Compared with their former regular dishes, what is left out in Cécile's current menu is the main dishes. Only with the arrival of Pierre and his deer haunch, the order of Cécile's table or the order of the Auclairs' world, by extension, is restored (*LN* 632).

As for the several items the Auclairs still have—some wild rice left from last year, some carrots, preserves, soup and a bottle of heavy gold-colored wine from the South—it is no mere accident that they appear in this context. David Porter once commented that "any reader of Willa Cather's fiction soon discovers that topics introduced apparently in passing often prove significant" (*DCA* 32). In the case of Cather's narration of soup, the most memorable soup that comes to readers' mind is

Father Latour's famous comments on Father Vaillant's French onion soup in *Death Comes for the Archbishop*: "when one thinks of it, a soup like this is not the work of one man. It is the result of a constantly refined tradition. There are nearly a thousand years of history in this soup" (*DCA* 39).

While Father Vaillant's onion soup is read by Father Latour as a cultural emblem, an encoded script that embodies the long history and tradition of human beings, soup in *Shadows on the Rock* carries other meanings. First of all, like chocolate and conserves, soup is used as a marker of the privilege enjoyed by the Auclairs. The Pigeons, for instance, could supply as much bread as Blinker (who tends the oven fires for Nicholas Pigeon, the baker) could eat, yet Blinker is given no soup there. The real reason for this is not as it is claimed that "Madame Pigeon has too many children to feed" (*LN* 472). Instead it has a great deal to do with the social class of the Pigeons. The Pigeons, a baker's family, basically belongs to the lower middle class. Unlike the upper class families such as the Auclairs, people from working class tend to eat foods that are "simultaneously most 'filling' and most economical" because of "the necessity of reproducing labor power at the lowest cost" (Bourdieu, 1984: 177). Bread is that kind of food which is much more filling than some fluid food, such as soup. Also, the making of soup is less economical than the making of bread for it is often the case that in making soup, one takes more efforts and time. If we take these elements into account, it is no wonder that Blinker will get enough bread but no soup at the Pigeons' house.

Secondly, in *Shadows on the Rock*, all three generations of Auclairs women all offer hot soup to the socially miserable and the poor. Back in France, Cécile's grandmother often saved a cup of hot soup and a piece of bread for the poor old Bichet and here in Quebec; here both Cécile's mother and Cécile herself provide soup to Blinker. Since soup often recalls the images of mixing different ingredients together, giving others soup can be read as a gesture of showing concern for, sympathy with and even tolerance toward social outcasts. In *Shadows on the Rock*, soup is both a marker of social standing and a medium through which one can negotiate one's relationship with others.

Critical attention to Cather's references to wine is relatively rare when compared with critical attention to her usage of food, yet more often than not such references prove revealing and integral to her design (qtd. in Romines et al., 2010: 32). David Porter's essay "'I have some Champagne for You': Wine in Willa Cather's Fiction" gives a subtle interpretation of wine in Cather's fiction ranging from her early stories, such as "Paul's Case", to her mature works, such as *The Song of the Lark*, *A Lost Lady*, *The Professor's House* and *Death Comes for the Archbishop*. Porter's examination not only asserts that there is a strong association between Cather's use of wine and the recurrent motif in her works, but also points out the binary nature (or to use Porter's original word "wine's bimodality") of Cather's wine. For instance, in *Death Comes for the Archbishop*, wine can be associated on one hand with the civilized and civilizing ways that the two bishops bring to everything they do, and on the other hand with the "undisciplined drunkenness and uncivilized values of priests like Gallegos and Baltazar" (qtd. in Romines et al., 2010: 35). When compared with Porter's overview of the nature as well as the function of wine in Cather's fiction, Charmion Gustke's interpretation is more specific in his essay "Somewhere between Temperance and Prohibition: The Wandering Alcoholics in *The Song of the Lark*", he focuses on the role of alcoholism in Cather's one specific novel. Even though the image of wine reappears repeatedly in *Shadows on the Rock*, its role in the story has not been addressed fully.

In *Shadows on the Rock*, drinking wine is a common practice in the everyday life of the Auclairs' household. For their dinner, Mr. Auclair pours a glass of red wine for his little daughter and one of white for himself (*LN* 470). But on those rare occasions, such as when distinguished guests come to visit their house, Mr. Auclair would bring up a special bottle of wine from his cellar. In Father Hector's case, it was a bottle of "fine old Burgund", and in Pierre's case, it was "heavy gold-colored wine from the South" (*LN* 558-632). Pierre says to Mr. Auclair, "Let us cheer our hearts a little while we can. Good wine was put into the grapes by our Lord, for friends to enjoy together" (*LN* 633). Pierre's words point out the cultural function of wine: it is "the symbolic antisadness element, the festive face of the meal" (qtd. in de Certeau et al., 1998: 90).

Unlike other kinds of food, the discourse on wine is much more nuanced: the pleasure of drinking well always tends toward the boundary of drinking too much (qtd. in de Certeau et al., 1998: 88). In *Shadows on the Rock*, through the allusion to the drunken Indian, Cather cautions against the latent danger in overdrinking. Writing in August 1936 to her friend about Jobyna Howland, an actress who had just died after a long addiction to alcohol, Cather asked why people over-drink, when a little wine in moderation is so good (Stout, 2002: 196). In *Shadows on the Rock*, more than once Monsieur Auclair's friend Father Hector "had given a drunken Indian a good beating, and the Indian had come and thanked him afterwards, telling him he did quite right" (*LN* 557). The act of selling as much brandy as they want to the Indians is a demonstration of the Whites' attempt to dominate and absorb the Indians. Also, a seeming passing reference to the controversies over the "brandy traffic" between the governor and Saint-Vallier demonstrates that eating and drinking is about more than physical nourishment or sensual pleasure, sometimes it is about power. Here the power of the wine equals any major force: law, weaponry and nature. It is in this sense that Piatti-Farnell maintains that "starting from the physical dimension of the body, food can move into political, social, cultural and economic relations" (2011: 1).

Of Cather's works, *Shadows on the Rock* is clearly a case in point in which Cather makes good use of the discourse of eating to explore the rich meanings behind this simple physical act. In *Shadows on the Rock*, through the exploration of the substances, contents and habits of the Auclairs' daily consumption, Cather gives us clues about the social and cultural identity of the Auclairs. In *A Lost Lady*, a novella Cather published seven years prior to *Shadows on the Rock*, on the other hand, she draws our attention to the cultural meaning as indicated by the group members with whom one dines. Cather uses the shifting of characters that gathered around the same table to measure the passing of one old order and the coming of another.

First published in the year of 1923, *A Lost Lady* is one of Cather's classic novels about life on the Great Plains. Set between 1883 and 1893, a decade marked by "change heralded as progress" (Rosowski and Ronning, 1997: 192), the novel is a celebration of Marian Forrester, the eponymous heroine of the story. To be specific, it is a hymn to the courage and determination Marian showed in time of great changes

## Chapter III Doing-cooking

in the cultural milieu in which she lived.[①] In *A Lost Lady*, the tension created by the passing of one order and the emergence of another is defined by two dinner parties presided over by two major characters representing two time periods and two sets of values.

The two parties are set almost four years apart.[②] Despite Marian's complaint about the poverty they had just begun to experience, Niel Herbert remembers, as we readers do, the glittering elegance of the first party. Captain Forrester still makes a "commanding figure at the head of his own table, with his napkin tacked under his chin and the work of carving well in hand" (*ALL* 48). In addition to that, Captain Forrester performs the elaborate rituals of consideration and politeness (qtd. in Romines, 2010: 78). He meets his guests at the door. He offers a timely compliment to each of his guests. He speaks highly of Frank's serving of wine for everybody—"Very good, Frank, very good" (*ALL* 47). To his women guests, he is a gentleman to the last: "What part of the turkey do you prefer, Mrs. Ogden?" "Mrs. Forrester, what part of the turkey shall I give you this evening?" "Is smoke offensive to you, Mrs. Ogden?" "Is smoke offensive to you, Constance?" (*ALL* 48-56)

Nearly all the guests present at the first dinner party seem lovable with the exception of Constance Ogden. Despite her "unpardonably homely" countenance[③]

---

① Cather's model for Mrs. Forrester in *A Lost Lady* is Mrs. Garber of her hometown, Red Cloud. Yet Cather's writing contemporary to *A Lost Lady* shows that her feelings toward Mrs. Garber are remarkably similar to those she holds towards Mrs. Fields. Cather met with Mrs. Fields, the wife of the Boston publisher James T. Fields in 1908. Cather pays tribute to Mrs. Fields in her essay "The House on Charles Street", Rosowski and Ronning's opinion is that, Cather sees both a determination to defy their age in Mrs. Garber and Mrs. Fields: both resisting growing old, and both also resist changes in the cultural milieu in which they found themselves.

② Niel was nineteen years old when the first party was held. He went to Boston to begin coaching for his entrance examinations at the Massachusetts Institute of Technology the following year. He did not come home until two years later. Captain Forrester died in December of the year Niel came back home. Niel was once again invited to dine at Mrs. Forrester's home next May.

③ Attention should be given to the way Cather uses food as a metaphor to give us a vivid description of the appearance and the personality of her characters. For instance, Mrs. Ogden has a pear-shaped face. Another minor character, Thad Grimes, has a "catfish mouth".

and her irritating mannerisms, Mrs. Ogden seems "thoroughly amiable" (*ALL* 44). Mr. Ogden is a short, weather-beaten man of fifty, who speaks little during the dinner time and seems to like the idea of letting his wife and daughter steal the show (*ALL* 45). Yet he is very sensitive to the real beauty of Mrs. Forrester: Niel notices that "when Mrs. Forrester addressed him, or passed near him, his good eye twinkled and followed her" (*ALL* 45). He is very gallant deep in heart and he proves to be a true friend of the Forresters' when he tries to help to secure a special increase of pension for Mrs. Forrester after her husband passed away (*ALL* 149). Niel and his uncle are the only townspeople that have been invited to the Forresters' party, which indicates not only the particular relationship between the two families but also the distinguished social status of Judge Pommeroy had in the small town.[①] Apart from the Ogdens, Niel and his uncle, another guest is Frank Ellinger, who is noted among the strangers as a terribly fast young man yet a model son, for "he had been devotedly caring for an invalid mother" (*ALL* 50).

The second party is held half a year after the death of Mr. Forrester. Whereas the damask, the shaded candles and the silver dishes on the dinner table remain the same, the characters that have been invited to the dinner have changed. Without her husband's stolid presence, Mrs. Forrester is the ostensible host and organizer of the house. Ivy Peters, who had been sent out to the front porch in the early scene in which Niel falls off of a tree and is carried to the Forresters', acts as the true owner of the house. During the party, Ivy mixes and serves the cocktails as though he had always belonged there. Niel could take the place of Mr. Forrester at the head of the table and carve the roast ducks for the guests, but clearly he is neither a commanding figure nor does he enliven the atmosphere of the party. "He addressed them one after another with energy and determination; he tried baseball, politics, scandal, the corn crop. They answered him with monosyllables or exclamations. He soon realized that

---

[①] The novel also gives other evidence to show the prestigious social status that Niel and his uncle enjoy in the small town. To make good preparation for the party, Mrs. Forrester has to go to Judge Pommeroy to borrow Black Tom. On the occasion of the dinner for the Ogdens, the Judge could afford to engage "the liveryman to take him and his nephew over in one of the town hacks—vehicles seldom used except for funerals and weddings".

they didn't want his polite remarks; they wanted more duck, and to be let alone with it." (*ALL* 162)

Niel is of course only partly to blame for the awkward situation at the dinner table. Unlike the guests who were present at the first dinner party, the attendees of the second one consist of young men of a totally different class origin. Before the dinner, Mrs. Forrester tries to bring the lack of table manners of her young guests to Niel's attention. "Did you notice," she whispers to him, "how they hold their glasses? What is it they do to a little glass to make it look so vulgar? Nobody could ever teach them to pick one up and drink out of it, not if there were tea in it!" (*ALL* 160) Young men like Ivy Peters and Joe Simpson (he is one of the guests at the second party and he conducts a clothing business) are representatives of a new generation rising out of a world of economic exchange and commerce. They may take possession of great wealth, yet as far as "refined tastes, manners, and habits of life" are concerned, they may need more time to cultivate those (Veblen, 2007: 36).

When pairing these dinner parties together, we see that, for the first generation of guests, they are occasions to mourn the passing of the good old days, to celebrate friendship and to engage in wit conversation; for the new generation, dinner parties are just opportunities to appease one's hunger. "Dinner was soon over, at any rate. The hostess's attempts to prolong it were unavailing. The salad and frozen pudding were dispatched as promptly as the roast had been." (*ALL* 162) Niel concludes that "a beefsteak with potatoes would have pleased them better! They didn't really like this kind of food at all" (*ALL* 162). The vulgar taste and manners of these nouveau riches evidently form a sharp contrast with the refined taste and manners of the old generation. In Niel's opinion, despite Mrs. Forrester's efforts to take the occasion of this dinner party to instill good manners into these young men, they clearly would not live up to her expectations.

Though grounded in the physical dimension of the body, food also fits into aesthetic, political and cultural frameworks. Wendy Leeds-Hurwitz argues that food serves "as an indicator of social identity, from region to ethnicity, from class to age or gender" (1993: 90). An exploration of Cather's representation of doing-cooking in her major works, *O Pioneers!, My Ántonia, Shadows on the Rock* and *A Lost*

*Lady*, reveals the rich cultural meanings of Cather's discourse on food. In Cather's works, doing-cooking is "a vehicle for artistic expression, a source for sensual pleasure, an opportunity for resistance and even power" (Heller and Moran, 2003: 6). The explorations of the paradoxical and subtle relationship between gender and cooking, the practice of art and doing-cooking, doing-cooking and the past, and the politics involved in the preparation and consumption of food testify to the shifting and malleable nature of this seemingly common practice of everyday life. More importantly, they demonstrate Cather's capability in extracting meaning from such a simple act of everyday life.

# Chapter IV
# The Act of Storytelling

While the former two chapters focus on the study of the practice of everyday life—"the practice of neighborhood" and "doing-cooking" in Cather's major works—this chapter moves to explore another important part of Cather's construction of the everyday life, which is "storytelling". Whereas the theoretical frameworks for Chapter Two and Chapter Three both originate from the second volume of *The Practice of Everyday Life*, the theoretical framework for this chapter is derived from de Certeau's discussion of the act of narration and storytelling in particular, in the first volume of *The Practice of Everyday Life*.

In general, de Certeau's account of the practice of everyday life revolves around a series of activities and spheres of practices—walking, reading, telling stories, all of which he regards in his text as analogues to one another. In *The Practice of Everyday Life*, whenever storytelling is invoked, it is often interwined with de Certeau's discussion of the act of narration. Narrative, for de Certeau, covers a wide range of different practices, and storytelling is only one of the many common practices of de Certeau's narrative. The act of narration, or telling a story, appears in several places in *The Practice of Everyday Life*. De Certeau's main points concerning the relationship between storytelling and everyday life are as follows:

> Tales and legends are deployed in a space outside of and isolated from daily

competition, that of the past, the marvelous, the original. In that space can thus be revealed, dressed as gods or heroes, the models of good or bad ruses that can be used every day. (1984: 24)

...

"Stories" provide the decorative container of a narrativity for everyday practices. (1984: 71)

...

Narration [the same can be applied to storytelling] belongs to the art of making a coup: it is a detour by way of a past ("the other day" "in olden days") or by way of a quotation (a "saying", a proverb) made in order to take advantage of an occasion and to modify an equilibrium by taking it by surprise. Its discourse is characterized more by a way of exercising itself than by the thing it indicates. And one must grasp a sense other than what is said. It produces effect, not objects… It is an art of saying… Something in narration escapes the order of what it is sufficient or necessary to know, and, in its characteristics, concerns the style of tactics. (1984: 80)

...

The story does not express a practice. It does not limit itself to telling about a movement. It makes it. One understands it, then, if one enters into this movement oneself [that's to say to play it out in one's own way]… [And to enjoy] the pleasure of storytelling… The storyteller falls in step with the lively pace of his fables. He follows them in all their turns and detours, thus exercising an art of thinking. (1984: 82)

To sum up, stories describe and comment on the performance of everyday practices. Yet they do not limit themselves to that function. As de Certeau has always emphasized throughout his project, the significance of storytelling to everyday life lies in what can be made out of the practice of storytelling. Storytelling creates models of "tactics, ruses and coups" that can be employed by both storytellers and audiences in their everyday lives. It is in this sense that narration or the act of storytelling is "an art of saying" or "an art of thinking", which means that writers and storytellers alike can employ it to express their views on everyday life.

Cather attaches great importance to the art of storytelling. Speaking of the beginning of her impulse to write, Cather expresses candidly her admiration for her immigrant neighbors, who can somehow manage to tell her a great many wonderful stories about the old country from which they have emmigrated (qtd. in Bohlke, 1986: 10). Strongly influenced by her earlier education, Cather's fiction is filled with the pulse of oral narrative, which is evident not only in her preference for episodes over plot-driven details (Driedger, 2007: 353), but also in her narrative technique of inserting stories into stories (McDonald, 1998: 14). Both the influence of storytelling on Cather's development as a writer and the importance of storytelling to her works have been much explored by recent scholars, such as Mildred Bennett, Richard H. Millington, Derek Driedger, Susan J. Rosowski, Evelyn I. Funda, Lisa Marie Lucenti and Ann Romines.

As far as the act of storytelling in Cather's works is concerned, scholars tend to focus on either the act of storytelling as a "distinctive narrative practice" (Millington, 1994: 695) or the act's function as a dynamic process of negotiation and reciprocity, leading from individualism to involvement, intimacy and ultimately to community (Funda, 1998: 53). These studies attest to the significance of storytelling both as a stylistic feature and thematic concern of Cather's aesthetics. Yet none of these studies have attempted to interpret storytelling from the particular perspective of everyday life, nor are there detailed studies focusing on the exploration of the interactions between storytelling and other forms of everyday activities, such as cooking, quilting and housekeeping. The interpretation of the interplay between storytelling and other everyday life practices helps to further the understanding of the complexities of Cather's everyday life.

This chapter analyzes the multi-layered meaning of storytelling in *Death Comes for the Archbishop* and *My Ántonia*. In *Death Comes for the Archbishop*, storytelling is both the narrative style and the subject matter of the novel. By presenting readers with the (actual, imagined or partly imagined) life of Father Latour and all those related to him, Cather offers truth instead of facts in this novel. As for Cather's inset stories, while they originate from diverse sources and cover a wide range of genres, they share an investment in the dark side of human experience, including feelings such as pain, horror and death, as in the cases of *My Ántonia*.

## 4.1 Everyday Life Narration in *Death Comes for the Archbishop*

Of Cather's many novels, *Death Comes for the Archbishop* is among the most candidly and deliberately experimental in form (E. A. Bloom and L. D. Bloom, 1962: 479). Upon its first publication, Cather received hundreds of letters inquiring about her sources of the origins of the novel. Unable to reply personally to all of these inquiries, Cather sent an open letter to the editor of *The Commonweal*, telling him how she had become infatuated with the story of the Church and the Spanish missionaries during her stay in the Southwest, how she had intermingled her personal experiences with a book she had found that was written by William Joseph Howlett, *The Life of the Right Reverend Joseph P. Machebeuf* and came up with the story of the first bishop of New Mexico, Archbishop Lamy.

In this often-quoted letter to *The Commonweal*, Cather provides an answer as to the models from which she draws her inspiration for the creation of *Death Comes for the Archbishop*. Preferring the term narrative to that of novel, Cather confesses that throughout her life, she had wanted to write something in the style of a legend:

> Since I first saw the Puvis de Chavannes[①] frescos of the life of Saint Genevieve in my student days, I have wished that I could try something a little like that in prose; something without accent, with none of the artificial elements of composition. In the Golden Legend the martyrdoms of the saints are no more dwelt upon than are the trivial incidents of their lives; it is as though all human experiences, measured against one supreme spiritual experience, were of about the same importance. The essence of such writing is not to hold the note, not to use an incident for all there is in it—but to touch and pass on. (*WCW* 10)

Cather's disclosure of her intention to write *Death Comes for the Archbishop* in the

---

[①] Pierre Puvis de Chavannes (1824-1898) is the French painter, who becomes the president and co-founder of the National Society of Fine Arts and whose works influence many other artists. His two subjects on Saint Geneviève are *L'Education de Sainte Geneviève* and *La Vie Pastoral de Sainte Geneviève*.

Chapter IV The Act of Storytelling

form of a legend suggests an important parallel with what de Certeau says about the nature of narration. According to de Certeau, narration is basically an art of saying designed to produce an effect. Instead of reading word by word, an ideal reader is expected to grasp a sense from the narration, for "something in narration escapes the order of what it is sufficient or necessary to know, and, in its characteristics, concerns the style of tactics" (1998: 80).

In his mural of the life of Saint Genevieve, Puvis means to let the figure of Genevieve set the tone for the whole scene. For this reason, instead of clearly portraying Genevieve or his duties, in his mural Puvis simply hints at the existence of Genevieve through the presence of the sheep. Meanwhile scattered throughout the painting are detailed images representing everyday life: a young girl kneels down, praying in front of a crudely made cross tied to the trunk of a tree; a woman nestles a baby in her arms; a man places a cluster of twigs at his feet; a peasant yokes his oxen so that they are ready for planting. In *Death Comes for the Archbishop,* Cather attempts to achieve what Puvis has done in his painting. While she infuses the narrative with her main character's presence, she does not allow the narrative to be taken over by the bishop, so that each action involves him.

Following the example of the frescoes and the legends, Cather constructs her novel as a series of short stories. While the main plot of the novel chronicles how Father Latour—sometimes single-handedly, other times together with his companion Father Vaillant—extends their mission into new territory, the subplots of the novel incorporate other characters. In *Death Comes for the Archbishop*, Father Latour functions much like the figure of Genevieve as seen in Puvis's fresco. In other words, even though Latour is not the central character

Figure 1 Pierre Puvis de Chavannes: Saint Genevieve as a child in prayer 1875-1876, oil on paper, 136.5×76.2 cm, signed and inscribed at lower left: au Comte Joseph Primoli affectuesement P. Puvis de C, Amsterdam, Van Gogh Museum, picture from Keeler 121.

by the standards of plotdriven novels, he is the very person who draws together the disconnected pictures and incidents of the whole book (qtd. in O'Connor, 2001: 349). In *Death Comes for the Archbishop*, Cather's intention of telling so many stories, be they myths, legends, hagiography, personal histories, miracles, folklores or adventures, is not to evoke suspense. Rather, it is in service of "a massive cumulative intention" (E. A. Bloom and L. D. Bloom, 1962: 479), which is to convey to readers the mood and the spirit in Father Machebeuf's letters regarding the earlier saints— saints who accept the accidents and hardships of a desert country, relying on "joyful energy" to keep them going (*WCW* 10).

To achieve this effect, Cather designs *Death Comes for the Archbishop* as a group of stories relating to the life of the bishop. Movement in the book is just like that of a viewer moving from picture to picture, from panel to panel (Keeler, 1965: 253). Cather's propensity to insert stories into her main plot that seem irrelevant to the overall narrative arc has caused great controversy. Opinions vary on this stylistic choice. Take two of the most discussed texts, *My Ántonia* and *Shadows on the Rock*, as examples. On one hand, scholars such as Rene Rapin and David Daiches consider the disappearance of the heroine Ántonia in the middle part of *My Ántonia* a structural fault of the novel. On the other hand, scholars such as Richard H. Millington and Derek Driedger defend Cather against such charges, turning readers' attention to Cather's experimentation with the form of her novels and her thematic concerns. In these analyses, scholars explore in detail not only the book's narrative structure, but also its content. Reading *My Ántonia* in light of Walter Benjamin's 1926 essay "The Storyteller", in "Willa Cather and the 'The Storyteller': Hostility to the Novel in *My Ántonia*", Millington contends that storytelling in *My Ántonia* is both Cather's particular stylistic arrangement and an act of art. In a similar vein, Deborah Carlin's essay "Tales of Telling and Fictions of History: Casting *Shadows on the Rock*", not only makes a strong argument for the blurring of boundaries between fiction and history, but also gives a categorized analysis of the stories in *Shadows on the Rock*.

Compared with what has been achieved in the study of both *My Ántonia* and *Shadows on the Rock* in terms of the significance of storytelling both as subject matter and narrative device, the analysis of storytelling in *Death Comes for the*

*Archbishop* is remarkably sparse. To be sure, even after its initial release, the book's "episodic construction" generated much controversy, as critics puzzled over its proper generic classification—Is it a history, a novel, or as the author claimed, is it simply a "narrative"? (Randall III, 1960: 250). Debates over the genre of the text also gave rise to discussions as to the reliability of the narrative. Henry Longan Stuart, for instance, expressed his concern regarding Cather's tendency to dispense with the tyranny of fact, which has long been considered one of the conventions of the historical novel (qtd. in O'Connor, 2001: 312).

Critics such as Edward A. Bloom and Lillian D. Bloom, however, maintain that Cather's concern in *Death Comes for the Archbishop* is not with facts per se, but with how facts "through their symbolic or metaphorical nature convey elevated concepts" (1955: 505). Studies such as those above mentioned recognize the salient stylistic features of *Death Comes for the Archbishop*, each analyzing the ambiguities incurred by Cather's experimentation with the form of her book. Yet none of these analyses has attempted to make a connection between Cather's experimentation with her inset stories in *Death Comes for the Archbishop* in the way that Millington has with *My Ántonia* or Deborah Carlin with *Shadows on the Rock*. The study of the narrative structure and the content of the narrative of these inset stories is of great significance, for it sheds lights on the understanding of the accumulated controversy over the genre and the truth debates on the book.

In my study of those interlacing stories in Cather's *Death Comes for the Archbishop*, I find Deborah Carlin's essay "Tales of Telling and Fictions of History", abundantly rewarding in helping to trace out in great detail the significance of storytelling both as a narrative strategy and subject matter in *Death Comes for the Archbishop*. Analyzing the stories in *Shadows on the Rock*, according to the perspectives through which the narratives are narrated, Carlin divides these stories appearing in *Shadows on the Rock* into four categories: the first three narrative constructions in the text are narrated from the perspective of an external focalizer[1]

---

[1] Carlin borrows the term external focalizer from Mieke Bal, which means the "anonymous agent, situated outside the fibula".

while the fourth is focalized through a character in the story. Stories narrated by the same external focalizer can be subdivided into three groups in accordance with various levels of narration. The external focalizer may function as the agent who relates the primary narrative.[①] In *Death Comes for the Archbishop*, the opening line of the text is just such a construction: "One afternoon in the autumn of 1851 a solitary horseman, followed by a pack-mule, was pushing through an arid stretch of country somewhere in central New Mexico" (*DCA* 17). In this instance, the external focalizer provides readers with a view on the time, the main character and the geographical location of the story.

At the second level of narration, the external focalizer coincides with one character of the story, who happens to have access to the story of another character. For instance, in Book Nine of the text, many stories of the blessed experiences of the early Franciscan missionaries are related to readers by the external focalizer through the memory of Father Latour:

> When, as a young man, Father Latour first went down into Old Mexico... he had met on his journey priests... who related many stories of the blessed experiences of the early Franciscan missionaries.
>
> ...
>
> One night in his travels through Durango, Father Latour was entertained at a great country estate where the resident chaplain... told a story of this same Father Junipero. (*DCA* 278-279)

That the story of Father Junipero is repeatedly retold and reheard (later by Father Latour himself on two different occasions) is an indication of how the retelling of the story of Father Junipero helps Father Latour sustain his faith in God in a wild area such as New Mexico.

The third level of narration appears when the story of a particular character is

---

[①] The primary narrative of *Death Comes for the Archbishop* is about how Father Latour accomplishes his mission in Santa Fe.

Chapter IV  The Act of Storytelling

related through the external focalizer, as in the following passages:

> It was said that this people had from time immemorial kept a ceremonial fire burning in some cave in the mountain. (*DCA* 122)
>
> ...
>
> It was common talk that Padre Martinez had instigated the revolt of the Taos Indians five years ago. (*DCA* 139-140)
>
> ...
>
> There was gossip about the lady in Santa Fe, of course, since she had retained her beautiful complexion and her husband's devoted regard for many years. (*DCA* 178)

In the above passages, the external focalizer not only focalizes the narrative, but also sets up a "superstructure of narratability within the text by retelling tales that have been told, and by telling tales as they are being told" (Carlin, 1992: 64). In Carlin's interpretation of the tales of *Shadows on the Rock*, common talk or gossip does not play a role as significant as it does here in *Death Comes for the Archbishop*. This suggests the distinctive methods Cather employs in these two texts. In her letter to *The Commonweal*, she admits candidly that she has all her life wanted to do something in the style of legend (*WCW* 9). In *Death Comes for the Archbishop*, a great number of the interwoven stories are about customs and folklore spreading among local people. Cather is very cautious when addressing rumor or common superstitions, and in most cases, she points that out (Bloom, E. A., 1955: 505).

Take, for example, the legends of Snake Root. Initially they are introduced to readers through the direct focalization of the external focalizer. Readers subsequently have access to Orchard's version of the "dark legends" through the language of the external focalizer— "Orchard confirmed the Father Latour that the legend about the undying fire was unquestionably true; but it was kept burning, not in the mountain, but in their own pueblo... About the snake stories, he was not certain" (*DCA* 134). Later on, the external focalization becomes an internal focalization, when the story is narrated by Orchard himself and is told as a story: "I remember something that happened when I was a little fellow. One night..." (*DCA* 135) In this case, the story is both within and apart from the primary narrative (Carlin, 1992: 64). These multiple layers of stories are also carried to other parts of the book. For instance, woven into the story of Padre Martinez are stories of Trinidad Lucero and the scandal of Father Lucero. In a similar vein, within the story of Don Antonio, there is also the story of Don Manuel Chavez. In each case, multiple layers of narration intermingle with one another.

Useful as Carlin's method of division is for the understanding of the inner structure of these stories, it represents only one approach to categorize the stories in *Death Comes for the Archbishop*. Stories in *Death Comes for the Archbishop* are very diverse. Some are about the customs of local people, others are adventure stories. A special group of stories concentrate on the everyday life of missionary priests. As foreshadowed in the prologue of the book, stories related to the daily life of these missionary priests exist to form a parallel as in the story of the missionary priest in the prologue and the story of Father Junipero, or a sharp contrast as in the story of Fray Baltazar, Padre Martinez, Father Lucero and Trinidad Lucero, with the everyday life of Father Latour.

The prologue of the book is about three worldly cardinals dining around a table where they are joined by an earnest missionary. Detailed attention to the complexion and dinner manners of these four diners reveals differences in dispositions and lifestyles of these missionaries. Whereas the sophisticated old world cardinals are surrounded by the comforts of life, the missionary priest who comes back from the wilderness lives a much simpler and more austere life: "His diocese lay within the icy arms of the Great Lakes, and on his long, lonely horseback rides among his missions the sharp winds had bitten him well" (*DCA* 6). In the middle of the dinner, the Spanish cardinal relates a story about how one bishop from New Spain carried off his great-grandfather's best painting and was never heard from again. After the story, the host leads his guests to the terrace. As they walk up and down the promenade, watching the stars come out, their talk touches upon many matters: a new opera by Verdi; the case of a Spanish dancing-girl who has recently turned religious and is said to be working miracles in Andalusia (*DCA* 14). By the end of the prologue, Father Latour's appointment has been assured, leaving much space for discussion as to what will happen to him in the wilderness.

Such is what has happened in the prologue of *Death Comes for the Archbishop*. Neither the three worldly cardinals nor the old missionary priest will ever appear again in the remaining parts of the book. It seems that the prologue merely exists to ensure Father Latour's appointment to his duty and to inform readers of the hardships that he will have to go through. For instance, "He will eat dried buffalo meat and frijoles with chili, and he will be glad to drink water when he can get it. He will have no easy life… That country will drink up his youth and strength as it does the rain. He will be called upon for every sacrifice, quite possibly from martyrdom" (*DCA* 10). Yet the significance of the prologue reaches far beyond this. On one hand, the prologue helps to set both the tone and the framework for the whole book. Like what has happened in the prologue (nothing dramatic but table talk), the remaining part of the book is nothing but an exploration of the daily life of Father Latour—his friendship with Father Vaillant, his encounter with the customs and folklores of the Mexicans and Indians, his ruminations about the beginning of his missionary life, and the activities in his diocese during his period of governance. On the other hand, differences in the disposition and the lifestyle between the austere missionary priest and the three worldly cardinals foretell the sharp contrast between Father Latour and the other notorious priests of the story.

In recounting the life story of Father Latour, Cather often chooses to depict the priest's moments of calm reflection. Yet when it comes to her characterization of figures such as Fray Baltazar, Padre Martinez, Father Lucero and Trinidad Lucero, what she chooses to concentrate on is the moments of carnival and violence. What happens to these persons is quite carnivalesque and the events jolt readers out of their normal expectations of priesthood.

"The Legend of Fray Baltazar" is inserted in Book Three of *Death Comes for the Archbishop*. Father Latour hears the legend of Fray Baltazar from Father Jesus during his mission to the Indian communities. Contrary to one's normal expectations of priesthood, Fray Baltazar "lived more after the flesh than after the spirit" (*DCA* 106). The poverty of cooking materials at the end of the world has proved an incentive for him to improve his diet (*DCA* 108). A local priest, Fray Baltazar does not live for his people, rather, he is a plunderer. For instance, he takes from his parishioners the best corn, beans and squash for his own table. Likewise, whenever his residents slaughter a sheep, the choicest portions go to his table. In addition, he exacts a heavy tribute in labor with the local women being enslaved to water his garden every evening (*DCA* 104).

The Acoma people silently bear Baltazar's tyranny until he accidentally kills one of his serving-boys. The tragedy happens in the week after St. John's Day when Baltazar invites the Padres from the neighborhood to his dinner party. Everything goes smoothly until the serving-boy spills a stream of rich brown gravy over one of the guests' head and shoulders. Baltazar is a quick-tempered person, and the brandy he drinks further leads him to lose his mind: "He caught up the empty pewter mug at his right and threw it at the clumsy lad" (*DCA* 110). The boy is struck to death, a tragedy which touches the bottom line of the local Indians. As a consequence, they overthrow Baltazar.

Attention should be paid as to how Cather buries violence in the seemingly tranquil daily life of Baltazar, and in his fascination with eating in particular. The atmosphere of the party initially seems to be peaceful: the host has taken extravagant pains with the dinner and his efforts are well recognized by the guests, who admit that they "had never sat down to food like that which rejoiced them to-day in the cool refectory, the blinds open just enough to admit a streak of throbbing desert far below them" (*DCA* 108-109). Both host and guests are in a good mood. When the priest from Isleta tells a funny story, the company laughs uproariously. Yet with one thing leading to another, what is laughable at first turns out to be disastrous in the end. It is ironical that the gravy that Baltazar has spared no effort to make proved to be his undoing (*DCA* 111).

As if such ridicule is not enough, Cather goes further in portraying the psychological state of the Padre before he meets his doom. Friar Baltazar feels, "indeed, very remorseful and uncomfortable, also indignant with his departed guests. For a moment he entertained the idea of following them; but temporary flight would only weaken his position, and a permanent evacuation was not to be thought of" (*DCA* 111). A permanent escape is not to be thought of because "his garden was at its prime, his peaches were just coming ripe, and his vines hung heavy with green clusters" (*DCA* 111). Forming a contrast with the gamut of emotions he has experienced, Baltazar notices that "the pueblo down there was much too quiet. At this hour there should be a few women washing pots or rags, a few children playing by the cisterns and chasing the turkeys. But today the rock top baked in the fire of the sun in utter silence, not one human being was visible" (*DCA* 111). This silence is of course a prelude to the tempest that is fast approaching.

Apart from the description of Baltazar's psychological activities, Cather also uses the change in nature to signal the advent of the impending disaster. As the sun sinks lower and lower, the silence is finally broke up by the "singing murmur of male voices from the pueblo below" (*DCA* 112). Baltazar understands clearly what awaits him ahead. Frightful stories of the torture of the missionaries during the great rebellion of 1680 flash through his mind: "One Franciscan had his eyes torn out, another had been burned, and the old Padre at Jamez had been stripped naked and driven on all fours about the plaza all night, with drunken Indians straddling his back, until he rolled over dead from exhaustion" (*DCA* 112).

What has happened to his forerunners seems to foretell Baltazar's destiny. When the moon rises, Friar Baltazar's fate is eventually sealed. The punishment is carried out in silence. The Indians walk silently across the rock to the loggia. When the friar inquires of them as to their activities, they made no reply. After the friar is caught, he does not supplicate or struggle. When he is swung out over the rock edge and back a few times, "no sound but hissing breath came through his teeth" (*DCA* 113).

Compared with Friar Baltazar, the figure of Padre Martinez in *Death Comes for the Archbishop* is more of a round character. While Baltazar is notorious for his insatiable appetite for food, Martinez is infamous for more than one thing. It is commonly known that Padre Martinez has instigated the revolt of the Taos Indians and makes a profit from the affair (*DCA* 140). Moreover, he openly flaunts the code of celibacy: it is rumored that his secretary Trinidad Lucero is his illegitimate son, and that a devout Mexican girl has been debauched by him. Yet from the same man, Father Latour hears the most impressive Mass sung. Martinez, in the bishop's opinion, represents talent corrupted by unhealthy desires. Cather describes Martinez in detail as the embodiment of animalistic since nobody passed him on the street without feeling his great physical force and his imperious will. Being an enormous man, "his broad high shoulders were like a bull buffalo's... the full lips thrust out and taut, like the flesh of animals distended by fear or desire" (*DCA* 140-141). Furthermore, when he goes to sleep, he snores like an enraged bull.

This combination of animal and human forms is a salient feature of carnival images and one of the most ancient grotesque forms mentioned in Bakhtin's *Rabelais and His World*. According to Bakhtin, carnival images often involve the playful combination of animal, vegetable and human forms, or the metamorphosis of one into another, and the body as depicted in grotesque realism is thus not an autonomous, self-sufficient object (1983: 67-68). Of all the features of Martinez's face, his mouth draws the greatest attention. Martinez's mouth is "the very assertion of violent, uncurbed passions and tyrannical self-will; the full lips thrust out and taut, like the flesh of animals distended by fear or desire" (*DCA* 141). When he laughs, "laughing did not become him; his teeth were too large—distinctly vulgar" (*DCA* 148).

The mouth is emphasized because it is in Bakhtin's view, the most important of all human features for the grotesque. In other words, the mouth dominates all else. Other features of the body—the head, ears and nose—are only frames encasing this wide-open bodily abyss (*DCA* 317). Bakhtin's elaboration makes plausible why when Cather introduces Trinidad Lucero, who is the Padre's illegitimate son, she gives her attention to the description of Trinidad's mouth. "The corners of his mouth were deep folds in plumpness, like the creases in a baby's legs." (*DCA* 145)

Trinidad Lucero is certainly another carnival figure in *Death Comes for the Archbishop*. When he makes his initial appearance in the novel, he is fast asleep on the floor of Martinez's study, woken up only after Martinez gives him a no very gentle kick in the ribs and then flees in panic (*DCA* 143). Subsequently, he said not one word during supper, but ate as if he were afraid of never seeing food again. After witnessing his table manners, Father Latour says this student gives the impression of being always stupefied by one form of sensual disturbance or another (*DCA* 145). The carnival spirit of Trinidad is likewise reflected in his fetish for religion. During the Passion Week, he tries to model the savior and has himself crucified. Yet "he is so heavy that after he had hung there a few hours, the cross fell over with him... he had himself tied to a post and said he would bear as many stripes as our savior—six thousand... But before they gave him a hundred, he fainted" (*DCA* 154).

In addition to Martinez and Trinidad, in the story of "the Miser", readers get a glimpse of Father Lucero, who is another of Cather's splendid portrayal of carnival characters in *Death Comes for the Archbishop*.① Old Marino Lucero has been a miser since his youth. His people love to tell "how he never bought anything, but picked up old brooms after housewives had thrown them away" (*DCA* 161). Marino has such a high fever for money that in his illness he is capable of killing a robber in a midnight scuffle.

Even though Trinidad and Marino are just minor characters in *Death Come for the Archbishop*, Cather renders them in such a wonderful way that they leave a deep impression on readers. Many critics agree that Cather's characterization in these cases is heavily influenced by Dante's work *The Divine Comedy*. To great extent, these characters are "personifications of one or another of the seven deadly sins—Father Martinez of lust, Father Baltazar of gluttony, Dona Isabella of female vanity and so on" (Wagenknecht, 1994: 111). Yet M. A. Stouck pinpoints another important possible source for Cather's characterization. In his opinion, *Death Comes for the Archbishop* has a more direct connection with Chaucer's *Canterbury Tales* and *The Divine Comedy* (1972: 532). Stouck's contention is well founded and the many parallels he finds between characters from *Canterbury Tales* and *Death Comes for the Archbishop* are appropriate. The carnival spirit of Cather's characters provokes laughter from readers, yet at the same time, such humor is "incongruous, ironic, absurd, or bizarre" (Harpham, 1976: 463).

In *Death Comes for the Archbishop*, Cather's preference for setting her stories in the remote past and adopting a storytelling mode not only causes some confusion as to the inner logic of her narrative, but also makes her vulnerable to criticism as

---

① Critic Edward Wagenknecht has long pointed out in *Willa Cather* that "the book (*Death Comes for the Archbishop*) is episodic far beyond the author's wont... there are separate stories, and there are stories within stories". In the novel, both the story of Trinidad Lucero and "the Miser" are within the story of Padre Martinez.

to the reliability and the contemporary relevance of her book. De Certeau contends that people enjoy the tales and legends of the remote past for they are "deployed in a space outside of and isolated from daily competition... In that space can thus be revealed... the models of good or bad ruses that can be used every day" (1984: 24).

However, Cather's tales and legends provide no models of good or bad ruses that can be reused in the every day. Granville Hicks once asked, "Does it touch our lives? Is this really the past out of which the present sprang? Did these men and women ever live? Is there anything in their lives to enable us better to understand our own?" (1967: 145) Clearly Cather did not write *Death Comes for the Archbishop* to be the kind of book that can live up to Hicks's standard. Art, Cather implies, in her response to Hicks in a letter to *The Commonweal* editor, is apolitical. Certainly there is no lack of tumult and fighting scenes in *Death Comes for the Archbishop* (the conflict between the white settlers and the Indians; the conflict between the friar and his parishioners and so on), yet the conflicts appear before the readers only dimly. In recounting the life story of Father Latour, for example, Cather may sometimes romanticize the daily life of her heroes at the expense of historical facts, yet she never exchanges human and experiential truth for those hard facts. After all, it is her belief that to set down a multitude of exact details about the physical and actual world would not in itself give a sense of life; rather it is "the verbal mood, the emotional aura of the fact or the thing or the deed, that gives high quality to the novel or the drama, as well as to poetry itself" (*SPW* 837). In summary, Cather's handling of the life story of Father Laotur in *Death Comes for the Archbishop*—she never trades human and experiential truth for hard facts, and the effect she has achieved— "to touch and pass on" define quite well her distinctiveness as a realist of everyday life. What is listed in the following can suggest how inset stories contribute to the function of storytelling in Cather's novels.

| Inset stories in *Death Comes for the Archbishop* | |
|---|---|
| 1 | The host—the Spanish cardinal—Garcia Maria de Allande, relates to his guests a story about his great-grandfather's painting. |
| 2 | Padre Herrera tells Bishop Latour and Father Vaillant of the miraculous appearance of the Blessed Virgin in the City of Mexico. |

(continued)

| | Inset stories in *Death Comes for the Archbishop* |
|---|---|
| 3 | Magdalena tells her story to the bishop, the notary, and St. Vrain. Since Magdalena speaks Spanish, her story is translated by St. Vrain for the audience. The external focalizer relates the story of Magdalena. |
| 4 | Father Valillant tells the bishop of the story of Fray Baltazar. The story of Baltazar is related to readers through the external focalizer. |
| 5 | The external focalizer relates the "dark legends" of Santa Fe. The trader, Orchard intervenes to provide his opinion and a description of his experience to the bishop. |
| 6 | The external focalizer relates the story of Padre Martinez. |
| 7 | Senora Carson tells the story of Trinidad Lucero to the bishop. |
| 8 | Father Joseph retells the scandal of Martinez he has heard to the bishop. |
| 9 | The external focalizer tells the story of Father Lucero, whose stories have become one of the legends of the countryside. |
| 10 | The external focalizer tells the story of Don Antonio. |
| 11 | The external focalizer tells the story of Manuel Chavez, who is one guest of Don Antonio's guests. |
| 12 | More than once Father Vaillant has spoken to the bishop of the story of Sada. There has been much whispering among the devout women of the parish about her pitiful case. The external focalizer relates the story of Sada. |
| 13 | Father Latour recalls an amusing story of Father Vaillant he has heard from Monsignor Mazzucchi. The external focalizer relates the story through Father Latour's memory. |
| 14 | The external focalzier relates the meeting of Father Latour and Father Vaillant through the memory of the former. |
| 15 | The external focalizer relates the story of the story of a prisoner named Ramon Armajillo through the memory of Father Valliant. |
| 16 | Father Latour recalls a miracle he has heard of from a resident chaplain about a miracle happened to Father Junipero. The external focalizer relates the story. |
| 17 | The external focalizer relates the beginning of Father Vaillant and Father Latour's missionary life. |
| 18 | The external focalizer relates the persecution of the Navajos and their exclusion from their own country through the memory of Father Latour. |

## 4.2 The Art of Storytelling in *My Ántonia*

Like *Death Comes for the Archbishop*, *My Ántonia* also contains multiple layers of stories and storytelling. While the primary narrative is chiefly about Jim Burden's telling of the stories of Ántonia, outside his stories, the introduction is narrated by an unnamed "I" (presumably the author herself), and within it are stories ranging from the story of Mr. Shimerda, to Pavel and Peter, Lena Lingard, Tiny Soderball, Mr. and Mrs. Cutter. The storytellers are as diverse as Jim, Ántonia, Pavel, Fuchs, Widow Steavens, Rudolph and Cuzak. Compared with the storytelling in *Death Comes for the Archbishop*, the storytelling in *My Ántonia* is much more extensive. A great number of scholars, such as Evelyn I. Funda, Pathula Wolley, Wilhite Keith and Annette Bennington McElhiney have elaborated upon the importance of storytelling as a narrative strategy in this novel. Both Funda and Wolley, for instance, read Cather's emphasis on storytelling as her way of endorsing Ántonia's perspective and privileging her experiences rather than those of the novel's professed narrator, Jim Burden's. Unfettered by debates about which narrative viewpoint is more reliable, in "Willa Cather and 'The Storyteller': Hostility to the Novel in *My Ántonia*", Richard H. Millington reads Cather's endorsement of meaning exemplified by the tradition of oral storytelling as a protest against the constriction of experience characteristic of modern life. Hence, this novel, in his opinion, invites us to understand "storytelling both as narrative form and as implying a stance toward experience, a way of life, a culture" (Millington, 1994: 689-691).

Millington's argument regarding the function of storytelling as a means through which the author shows her disagreement with the constriction of experience characteristic of modern life seems to contradict my conclusion concerning Cather's intention in writing *Death Comes for the Archbishop*—Cather's tales and legends reveal no models of good or bad ruses that can be reused every day. In fact, Millington's discussion of the act of oral storytelling as an alternative to the experiences associated with novel reading seems to have some affinity with de Certeau's discussion of the function of narrative to "describe and comment on the performance of everyday practices" (Highmore, 2002: 128). Yet this study argues that rather than being in conflict with my conclusion, Millington's celebration of the subversive nature of storytelling instead offers readers a completely different angle with which to read Cather's works. Millington's interpretation of the subversive nature of storytelling and its significance in giving meaning to the tediousness of everyday life begins and ends with the sharp contrast between oral storytelling and novel reading. In Millington's reading, even though he only makes sporadic reference to the context of storytelling, Millington subordinates any consideration of the role of the storyteller, as well as the function and nature of storytelling to his discussion of the sharp contrast between oral storytelling and novel reading.

*My Ántonia* is composed of multi-layered stories and storytelling. The foremost is Cather's story, the novel we read; however there is also Jim's telling of stories of persons with whom he happened to be familiar—these texts form the text that appears after the introduction (O'Brien, 2007: 7). In addition, there are a great number of other storytellers competing with Jim. This study focuses on the interpretation of inset stories told in the novel. By listing all of these inset stories told or retold in *My Ántonia*, this part of the chapter aims to identify the inner logic that links together all these disparate stories of Cather's fiction.

A close reading of the juxtaposition of these stories reveals one common attribute shared among diverse stories—they are often concerned with the dark side of human experience, or feelings such as pain, horror and death. Cather intermingles the act of storytelling with other harmless everyday activities such as cooking, eating and celebrating festivals so as to make readers feel more keenly that dark side of everyday life. On the whole, the bleakness and grotesqueness of these stories form a sharp contrast with the harmonious daily routines of everyday life, yet they also testify to the potential danger, violence and threats, which are inherent to everyday life.

In *My Ántonia*, apart from Jim Burden, Ántonia is the most active storyteller in the novel. In Susan Rosowski's view, in the novel, "the early male myths of adventure have led to pointless wandering and lonely exile, and the women, originally assigned roles of passivity, have become the vital sources of meaning" (1986: 91). In other words, even though Ántonia begins as the object of Jim's story, gradually she moves to the role of active storyteller. In the novel, Ántonia manifests her potential for storytelling immediately after she has mastered English as her second language. One afternoon after Ántonia and Jim have finished their reading lesson, Ántonia tells Jim two stories which are related to her part of the world. The first story is concerned with the terrific struggle between trained dogs and badgers— "Those dogs, she said, went down into the hole after the badger and killed him there in a terrific struggle underground; you could hear the barks and yelps outside. Then the dogs dragged himself back, covered with bites and scratches, to be rewarded and petted by his master" (*MÁ* 736).

Simple as this story is, it contains the seeds of all the major conflicts that will appear in the later part of the novel. For instance, the bloody fighting scene featuring the hunting-dog and the badger seems to foreshadow the brutal stories of Peter and Pavel, in which humans who beat hungry wolves yet are in fact beaten by the inhuman and barbaric sides of human beings themselves. The excitement and satisfaction humankind finds in witnessing the process of killing is later echoed in Jim's narration of his and the whole neighborhood's excitement regarding Mr. Shimerda's suicide.

Ántonia's story about Old Hata is provoked by the "thin, rusty little chirp" of a little insect (*MÁ* 736). The heroine of Ántonia's second story is concerned about an old beggar woman in her village at home, who went about selling herbs and roots she had dug up in the forest. Despite her poverty, this old woman is well loved and respected by the children, who not only "loved to see her coming and saved their cakes and sweets for her", but also called her "Old Hata" (*MÁ* 737). Even though only children are mentioned as the caretakers of Old Hata, Mr. Shimerda's tender feelings toward the green insect after he hears the name of Old Hata indicates that the old woman is, in fact, well taken care of by the whole community— "he untied the handkerchief, separated her hair with his fingers, and stood looking down at the green insect. When it began to chirp faintly, he listened as if it were a beautiful sound" (*MÁ* 738). The attention and care Old Hata has received form a sharp contrast with the alienation and loneliness that both Mr. Shimerda and the tramp will suffer from in Black Hawk.

The two Russians, Peter and Pavel, are two of the very few friends that Mr. Shimerda finds out in the new country. Even though Jim describes them as the strangest and the most aloof men among the first settlers, Ántonia finds them very nice. Thanks to them, Ántonia sees her father laugh (*MÁ* 733). Peter and Pavel

## Chapter IV  The Act of Storytelling

conduct a comfortable life in the new country until Pavel falls ill. On his deathbed, Pavel reveals to both Ántonia and her father a long story of his dark past. Cather narrates, "when Pavel and Peter were young, living at home in Russia, they were asked to be groomsmen for a friend who was to marry the belle of another village. It was in the dead winter and the groom's party went over to the wedding in sledges. Peter and Pavel drove in the groom's sledge, and six sledges followed with all his relatives and friends" (*MÁ* 748). The wedding turns out to be very successful for both the guests and the hosts are in good moods. Yet on their way back, they are chased by hundreds of hungry wolves. The driver of the last sledge loses control, and as a consequence, the occupants are devoured by the hungry wolves. What happens to the last sledge quickly happens to other sledges. When three big wolves get abreast of Pavel and Peter's horses, Pavel throws both the bride and the groom to the ravenous wolves.

Pavel's story of the wolves signals a special moment in the novel in which the ongoing routine of everyday life is interrupted by an element of the gothic. Cather embeds the story within the routine of everyday life, writing "One afternoon Ántonia and her father came over to our house to get buttermilk, and lingered, as they usually did, until the sun was low. Just as they were leaving, Russian Peter drove up" (*MÁ* 745). That is how the story begins. Yet the atmosphere in which the story is situated—the howling of the coyotes outside of the door, the delirious situation of the storyteller, as well as the distinct effects of tuberculosis on Pavel's ravaged body, all seem to alert readers to the fact that the forthcoming tale is no ordinary experience at all.

When Pavel tells his story to Mr. Shimerda, the language barrier prevents Jim from having esay access to the content of the story, Ántonia provides a few hints like "They are wolves, Jimmy," "It's awful, what he says!" Yet what Jim primarily witnesses is the accumulation of tension as the storytelling goes on. When Pavel starts to talk to Mr. Shimerda, his voice is scarcely above a whisper, yet as the story continues, what has begun as a whisper turns into a burst of rage— "The sick man raged and shook his fist. He seemed to be cursing people who had wronged him" (*MÁ* 747).

Pavel feels wronged because under the weight of brutal exigency, he has no other option but to follow his instinct of self-preservation. Pavel admits candidly that he does not remember exactly how he knocks the groom over the side of the sledge or how he throws the bride after the groom (*MÁ* 750). As a typical protagonist of the naturalist plot, Pavel is just "a pawn to multiple compulsions" (Abrams, 2010: 304). Under the same circumstances, anyone might have made the same decision as he had in that night. Yet circumstances force Pavel to be cast aside—by his own mother as well as his fellowmen—and haunted.

In the end, Pavel's story is translated by Ántonia to Jim. On their way back home, when they were lying in the straw, Ántonia relates as much of the story as she can (*MÁ* 748). Of all audience to Pavel's story, Ántonia is singled out as the one who could relate the story. Ántonia is chosen as the only qualified storyteller not simply because she is the only figure that can translate perfectly well Pavel's story from one language to another, but because she is the only person who is capable of giving a reliable narration of the dark history of Pavel and Peter.

Ántonia is an attentive listener. As Pavel tells his story, "Ántonia took my [Jim's] hand under the table and held it tight. She leaned forward and strained her ears to hear him" (*MÁ* 747). She likewise tries not to pass judgment on Pavel's behavior. Jim is too stimulated by the story to give a reliable account. After hearing that Pavel is going to talk to Mr. Shimderda and his daughter Ántonia, Jim entreats his grandmother to let him go with them, "I would gladly go without my supper, I would sleep in the Shimerdas' barn and run home in the morning" (*MÁ* 745).

Jim's eagerness and enthusiasm for what is going to happen over there for two Russians and his sense of pleasure after hearing Ántonia's retelling of the story indicate his yearning for something peculiar that is able to light up the dullness of everyday life. Pavel's story is heard not long after Jim and Ántonia's arrival at Black Hawk. Here is Jim's first impression of the place:

> There seemed to be nothing to see; no fences, no creeks or trees, no hills or fields. If there was a road, I could not make it out in the faint starlight. There was nothing but land: not a country at all, but the material out of which countries are made. No, there was

nothing but land… I had the feeling that the world was left behind, that we had got over the edge of it, and were outside man's jurisdiction. (*NS* 718)

Like the other inserted stories that disrupt the flow of *My Ántonia*'s main plot, Peter and Pavel's story renders narrative as an alternative to the tedious life of Black Hawk (Millington, 2005: 55). In *My Ántonia*, the story of Peter and Pavel serves as a warning of the latent danger and violence that could erupt at any moment of everyday life. The story also foreshadows the tragic destiny of Mr. Shimerda. Not long after his confession of his sin to Mr. Shimerda, Pavel dies and Peter "sold off everything, and left the country" (*NS* 750). The loss of his two friends has a depressing effect upon Mr. Shimerda. The onset of the big storm of the winter exacerbates the economic situation of the Shimerdas. With everything going from bad to worse, Mr. Shimerda eventually loses heart and kills himself.

Similar to the context in which Peter and Pavel's story is told, the story of how Mr. Shimerda commits suicide is also embedded in the daily activities of the storytellers. At first, Jake and Fuchs describe over coffee about how Mr. Shimerda has killed himself to Jim's grandfather (*NS* 775). Then, while Jake and Jim are washing dishes, Jake tells Jim about the state of things at the Shimerdas (*NS* 779). Later, the story of Mr. Shimerda's death is told by Jim and his grandmother to the Harlings when they pay a visit to their house. Of the three narrations, Jake's version lays more emphasis on the grotesque nature of Mr. Shimerda's killing—"The dead man was frozen through, 'just as stiff as a dressed turkey you hang out to freeze,' Jake said. The horses and oxen would not go into the barn until he was frozen so hard that there is no longer any smell of blood" (*NS* 779-780). Readers do not have access to what the Burdens have told to the Harlings about Mr. Shimerda's death, yet from Mrs. Harling's response—that the girl will be happy here, and she'll forget those things, one can infer that the Burdens' telling must have focused on the ugly details revolving around Mr. Shimerda's suicidal behavior too (*NS* 810).

Unlike Jake's and the Burdens' versions, Fuchs's narration of Mr. Harling's suicidal story, puts significant emphasis on the intricate relationship between the ongoing of daily routine and the outbreak of death and violence in the everyday life.

In Fuchs's story, till the last moment of his life, Mr. Shimerda had done everything natural. "He shaved after dinner, and washed himself all over after the girls had done the dishes...Then he put on a clean shirt and clean socks, and after he was dressed he kissed her and the little one and took his gun and said he was going out to hunt rabbits."(*MÁ* 776) The fact that death and violence are inextricably interwoven with the known and familiar intensifies the terror, for it indicates the unpredictability of everyday life.

Instead of being an occasion of mourning, Mr. Shimerda's accidental death gives people something to talk about, it also gives the daily life of the whole town an almost festival-like air. Jim notices that "now everyone seemed eager to talk" (*NS* 785). The postmaster, the brother of Widow Steavens and the father of the German family all come to the dining-room of the Burdens, inquiring about the suicide, while grandmother entertains the visitors with sugar-cakes and hot coffee. After the visitors depart, Otto Fuchs, fills the house with "the exciting, expectant song of the plane" (*NS* 784).

The death of Mr. Shimerda also prompts Otto to tell Jim tale after tale about the Black Tiger Mine (*NS* 785). Otto's tales of "violent deaths and casual burying" foreshadow what will happen to Mr. Shimerda's dead body. Jack and Jelinek "cut the body loose from the pool of blood in which it was frozen fast to the ground" (*NS* 787). As if such brute handling were not violent enough, Cather goes further to show how apathetic and indifferent the townspeople's reactions towards Mr. Shimerda's death are, characterizing—Mr. Bushy, the postmaster, and grandmother are sure that a man who had killed himself could not be buried in a Catholic graveyard and that even the Norwegians are unwilling to take Mr. Shimerda in (*NS* 784). On the day of the funeral, "everyone was afraid of another storm and anxious to have the burial over with" (*NS* 787). Such corrosive treatments of the dead dissolve any remaining sense of the funerary ritual as honoring the dead and asserting human dignity. They also shatter our frames for the social processing of death and subvert the idealism we have about human life.

Pondering over the possible reasons for the suicide of Mr. Shimerda, Jim confesses that he knows that "it was homesickness that had killed Mr. Shimerda"

(*NS* 779). Yet homesickness is certainly not the only reason for the violent death of Mr. Shimerda. To explain to readers who are to blame for the death of Mr. Shimerda, Cather arranges for Ántonia to tell the story of the wandering tramp. This tramp wanders along to ask for a job, is subsequently offered a job, but then only works for a few minutes before he "jump[ed] head-first right into the threshing machine" (*NS* 826). Like the telling of Peter and Pavel's story as well as Mr. Shimerda's suicide, the story of the tramp① is also embedded into the harmonious daily routine of the Harlings. It grows out of an ordinary conversation about the strenuous work in times of threshing wheat (Fryer, 1986: 284).

Ántonia tells this story to Jim, Mrs. Harling and children as they are "picking out kernels for walnut taffy" (*NS* 825). In the Harling's home, the suicidal story of the tramp is, like all the other stories that Ántonia has formerly told to the children (Mrs. Harling's little girl Nina often coaxed Ántonia to tell her stories about the calf that broke its leg, or how Yulka [Ántonia's younger sister] saved her little turkeys from drowning in the forest, or about old Christmases and weddings in Bohemia), supposed to be "a bedtime story" (Lucenti, 2000: 203). But the tramp's story is no innocent tale of lives saved by kind-hearted children or of joyful families gathering together to celebrate holidays or weddings. Instead, it is about a man driven to madness and suicide by his alienation from the whole community (Funda, 1999: 205). Moreover, the fact that the tramp singles Ántonia out as someone with whom to talk and make gestures — "he comes right up and begins to talk like he knows me already… he waved his hand to me and jumped head-first right into the threshing machine after the wheat"—makes this story analogous to the story of Mr. Shimerda's suicide (*NS* 825). It provokes readers to think about the possible link between the tramp's suicidal behavior and that of Mr. Shimerda's.

---

① The image of wandering tramp appears first in *The Song of the Lark*, in which a similar "ugly incident" occurs in Thea's hometown of Moonstone: A wandering tramp performs a show, offering to eat a rattlesnake for the donation of one dollar. After he is arrested for causing a disturbance, he took his revenge against the town by committing suicide by climbing into the water reservoir, thereby poisoning the water supply of Moonstone and causing the death of several adults and half a dozen children.

The curious artifacts the tramp leaves behind—a penknife, a wishbone and a piece of poetry, are clues that he has given people to interpret. Ántonia's continual bewilderment one year after the death of the tramp— "Wasn't that strange, Miss Frances…What would anybody want to kill themselves in summer for? In threshing time, too! It's nice everywhere then" (*NS* 826) indicates the failure of communication among human beings. In this sense, the story of the suicide of the tramp acts as a footnote to Mr. Shimerda's story. If Mr. Shimerda and the tramp are just as lucky as Old Hata, if they are also well taken care of by their community, they might not only survive in the harsh environment but also prosper in the new country.

The brutal story of Peter and Pavel, the suicide of Mr. Shimerda and of the tramp are only three of ugly stories in *My Ántonia*. *My Ántonia* is full of horror stories (Thompson, 2002: 146). The others include the villainy of Wick Cutter, Ántonia's seduction and betrayal, the miserable life of Ole Benson, among others. One common attribute of these stories is that they are often concerned with those dark sides of human experience, such as feelings of pain, alienation, horror and death. In general, the bleakness and grotesqueness of these stories form a sharp contrast with the seemingly harmonious daily routines of everyday life. Yet these stories also function to reveal the potential danger, violence and threat, which are inherent to everyday life.

Despite the ubiquity of these horror stories, *My Ántonia* is not on the whole a gloomy novel. In *The Song of the Lark,* in response to Thea's questioning about the whole town's apathy towards the pathetic tramp, Doctor Archie tells the young child, "ugly accidents happen, Thea; always have and always will. But the failures are swept back into the pile and forgotten. They don't leave any lasting scar in the world, and they don't affect the future. The things that last are the good things. The people who forge ahead and do something, they really count" (*NS* 415). Likewise, in *My Ántonia*, Cather affirms the power of people, such as Ántonia, who are able to weave the sadness of life into the web of ongoing life by telling stories (O'Brien, 2007: 7). What follows is the table that may suffice to illustrate the act of storytelling in *My Ántonia*.

# Chapter IV  The Act of Storytelling

| | **Inset stories in *My Ántonia*** |
|---|---|
| 1 | One afternoon when Ántonia and Jim are having their reading lesson on the warm, grassy bank where the badger lives, Ántonia relates to Jim stories of her own country: for instance, how a special kind of dog is trained to hunt the badger, and the story of an old beggar woman. |
| 2 | Standing in the middle of the kitchen floor, Ántonia tells the story of how Jim killed a rattlesnake with a great deal of color. |
| 3 | On his deathbed, Pavel tells a long story to Mr. Shimerda. On their way home, Ántonia tells Jim as much of the story as she can. |
| 4 | On bitter starlit nights, sitting around the old stove, Fuchs tells stories of outlaws and desperate characters he has known. |
| 5 | After Jake and Fuchs have swallowed their first cup of coffee, they begin to talk excitedly to Grandfather about the story of how Mr. Shimerda has killed himself. |
| 6 | While Jake and Jim are washing dishes, Jake tells Jim about the state of things at the Shimerdas. |
| 7 | On the occasion of Mr. Shimerda's death, everyone seems eager to talk. That afternoon after Fuchs makes Mr. Shimerda a coffin, he tells Jim story after story: about the Black Tiger Mine, violent deaths and casual burying, and the queer fancies of dying men. |
| 8 | Jim and his grandmother leave their supper dishes on the table to go to Mrs. Harling's house to hear about their visiting the Shimerdas. The Harlings beg the Burdens to tell them about Mr. Shimerda's death and the big snowstorm. |
| 9 | A young Dane, who has come to help the Burdens to thresh, tells Jake and Otto about how Lena put Ole Benson out of his head. |
| 10 | One evening when Jim and the Harlings are picking out kernels for walnut taffy in the kitchen, Ántonia tells a new story about a tramp she met when she was threshing last summer in the Norwegian settlement. |
| 11 | Jim and the hired girls go for a picnic. Ántonia tells stories of how her parents got married to her friends. |
| 12 | In Mrs. Burden's parlor, Mrs. Cutter tells the story of how her husband plotted against her. |
| 13 | Over coffee, Lena tells Jim of the story of Ole Benson. |
| 14 | After supper, in her old sitting-room, Mrs. Steavens tells Jim what happened to Ántonia after the courtship. |
| 15 | During his dinner in the Cuzaks, Rudolph tells Jim the story of Cutter's murderous attack on his wife to Jim. |
| 16 | After supper, when Cuzak and Jim take a stroll in the orchard and sit down by the windmill to smoke, Cuzak tells Jim about his life. |

# Chapter V
# Conclusion

Even though the majority of Willa Cather's works were composed in the period from the 1910s to the 1930s, her acquisition of her artistic skills began much earlier. This book argues that Cather's particular status as a writer at the turn of the twentieth century and her relationship with the literary imagination of the fin de siècle both serve as a determining element in her artistic development as a writer of everyday life. Her subject-matter indicates the strong influence of her childhood experience—Cather confessed that she had never found any intellectual excitement, any more intense that she used to feel when she spent a morning with of one her old women neighbors at her baking or butter making (qtd. in Bohlke, 1986: 10). The manner in which she chooses to present her material in her novels—her portrayal of new women figures in novels such as *My Ántonia, O Pioneers!* and *One of Ours*, her selection of topics in *Death Comes for the Archbishop* and *Sapphira and the Slave Girl*—embodies the way how she makes use of the interaction and interchange of a vortex of different ideas and forms of fin de siècle. A clear description of the cultural transformations under way during her apprenticeship years not only indicates her active engagement with American life, but also makes explicit her artistic practices and aesthetic commitments.

Following strictly the latest trend in Cather studies, this book is basically a textual analysis of Cather's representation of the geographical, the gendered as well as the artistic aspect of the practice of everyday life as they are inscribed and contested in her major works. Throughout this book, I maintain that Cather's narration of the practice of everyday life figures as a central element in the understanding of her aesthetics. To understand the complexity of her aesthetics of everyday life, first and foremost, we need to situate Cather in the cultural atmosphere of fin de siècle during which she received her literary training. Aestheticism, the New Woman and feminine writings and the question of realism are three of the main currents of radical and innovative thinking at the fin de siècle that are indispensable to the formation of Cather's aesthetics of everyday life. The debates and controversies centering on the main currents of fin de siècle not only supply her artistic models but also give embodiment to many of her deeply held values as reflected in her writings.

Cather appropriates what she finds accordant with her own artistic principles from the doctrine of aestheticism, but abandons what she finds inconsistent with her own. In this way she develops an aestheticism of a different type—a type of aestheticism that is deeply rooted in everyday life yet above the mundane routine of everyday experience. In her delineation of the common life of common people, Cather challenges the doctrines held by Wilde. In this way, she puts the term aestheticism to her own use. Cather's aestheticism transcends the exclusiveness of Wilde's aestheticism and becomes instead more comprehensive than what is initially advocated by the movement.

Fearing that identification with women writers would threaten her status as a true artist, Cather in her earlier literary career was constantly on guard against her female literary heritage. Sarah Orne Jewett becomes a key figure in helping Cather resolve the tension between the identities of woman and artist—the former associates her with traditional women's values "domesticity and nurturance", the latter with "public ambition, rule-breaking, and daring individualism" (Ammons, 1992: 123). Even though home plot and domestic ritual still occupy a significant place in her fiction, it is not the only yardstick against which her female characters are measured. Cather's characters such as Mr. Burdens and Mrs. Harling of *My Ántonia*, Mrs. Bergson of *O Pioneers!* and Old Mahailey of *One of Ours* are housewives in the most traditional sense of the word, yet without their sentimentality. Most of Cather's traditional housewives are tough immigrants, fighting harder to maintain the survival of their families in an alien land. In addition to these traditional housewives, in her works, novels and short stories alike, Cather also creates a large number of new women figures. Cather's new women figures, such as Alexandra Bergson, Tiny Soderball, Lena Lingard and Frances Harling, demonstrate the courage and grit of a new generation of professional new women.

Significant parallels could be easily drawn between Cather's relationship with aestheticism, with her female literary heritage and with realism. At first glance, Cather's enthusiasm for the depiction of everyday life activities, such as cooking and homemaking, bears much resemblance to that of the literary tradition of domestic fiction and realism, yet a close scrutiny reveals the distinctiveness of Cather's narrative strategies and thematic concerns. As far as the literary credos of realism are concerned, Cather finds much to dispute. In "The Novel Démeublé", Cather uses Balzac's overemphasis on the delineation of the trivial details of everyday life as a negative example to launch her own aesthetic principles—"The higher processes of art are all processes of simplification. The novelists must learn to write, and then he must unlearn it… to subordinate it to a higher and truer effect" (*NS* 836). True realist, in Cather's understanding, deals not just with mere verisimilitude, or simple facts—economic facts, biological facts and so on, but "uses those facts to point out a dimension beyond the real… it is writing that stirs one's imagination, that makes one dream" (Donovan, 1983: 102-103). Cather's handling of the life story of Father Laotur in *Death Comes for the Archbishop*—she never trades human and experiential truth for hard facts, and the effect she has achieved— "to touch and pass on" define quite well her distinctiveness as a realist of everyday life.

A literature review of Cather's interaction with the major literary movements of fin de siècle helps to show the bearing of the writer's historical moment on her artistic practice. Yet to have a comprehensive and thorough understanding of Cather's everyday life aesthetics, more theoretical support is needed. This discussion of Cather's everyday life has benefited a great deal from recent studies on everyday life, Michel de Certeau, Luce Giard and Pierre Mayol's two volumes of *The Practice of Everyday Life* in particular. De Certeau's elaboration on the relationship

## Chapter V Conclusion

between storytelling and everyday life, Mayol's discussion of the importance of the neighborhood as a spatial parameter for the understanding of the ongoing of everyday life as well as Giard's interpretation of both the gendered and the racial evocation of doing-cooking provide the theoretical framework for my chapters. A synthesis of these viewpoints helps to show the complexity of Cather's aesthetics of everyday life.

In the analysis of the neighborhood in Cather's fictions, three aspects call my attention. In revealing the dynamics of family and of the social system of the neighborhood of Back Creek in *Sapphira and the Slave Girl*, of Quebec in *Shadows on the Rock* and of Sweet Water in *A Lost Lady*, I intend to show the interlocking of race, power, sexuality and geography in Cather's diverse neighborhood. Both Thea's experience in Panther Canyon and Tom's memory of the Blue Mesa are based on Cather's journeys into the Southwest. Place rather than societal structure seems to be of more immediate concern to Cather in her two mesa novels. In telling Thea's and Tom's stories concerned with the place as well as with the lifestyle of the ancient people, I argue the significance of these places to the initiation of these two characters in Cather's works.

Cather's treatment of doing-cooking is an expression of her thematic concerns throughout her literary career. Doing-cooking is traditionally held to be the sphere of women and is usually relegated to a matter of no importance. In some of her works, Cather elevates cooking to the status of art, saving innumerable housewives from the anonymous. In others, such as *The Professor's House* and *One of Ours*, Cather also creates women characters who are determined not to be bound up in the kitchen and men figures who are quite devoted to cooking, thus subverting traditional concepts on the relationship between gender and cooking. The call of the past is strong in Cather's delineation of food in her major works. Cather's characters follow strictly their own particular way of cooking so as to make a distinction between their own culture and the others', as in the case of the mutual mistrust between Mrs. Burden and Mrs. Shimerda in *My Ántonia* and the superiority Cécile felt over the Harnois in *Shadows on the Rock*. In addition to the analysis of these culinary practices, this part of the present dissertation also argues that the "how, where and when" of eating in Cather's works, such as *Shadows on the Rock*, *My Mortal Enemy* and *A Lost Lady*, is used by the writer to convey the social status of the eaters and to measure the stability of the world.

In addition to the practice of the neighborhood and doing-cooking, in Cather's works, another aspect of everyday life that is explored in this book is storytelling. Storytelling is both the narrative style and subject matter of *Death Comes for the Archbishop*. By putting before readers the (actual, imagined or partly imagined) life of Father Latour and all those related to him, Cather offers us truth instead of facts. As for Cather's inset stories, they may originate from diverse sources and cover a wide range of genres, yet one common attribute shared among many of these stories is that they involve those dark sides of human experience, such as feelings of pain, horror and death as in the case of *My Ántonia*. In analyzing the functions and the characteristics of storytelling in these two novels, this book also examines the interactions between storytelling and other forms of everyday activities, such as cooking, quilting and housekeeping. The purpose of the examination of the interplay between storytelling and other forms of everyday life practices is to demonstrate the complexities of the aesthetics of Cather's everyday life.

The practice of the neighborhood, doing-cooking and storytelling are three of the most important but certainly not the only parameters to evaluate the significant role that everyday life plays in Cather's fiction. Moreover, in a sense, there is no strict dividing line among de Certeau's discussions of the act of storytelling as an art form and Mayol's and Giard's investigation of the other two distinctive fields of the practice of everyday life—living and doing-cooking. Hence we need a level of flexibility between chapters, in which the act of storytelling often happens in the process of cooking, and also particular social norms such as propriety apply to both the practice of the neighborhood and the practice of table manners.

Apart from these three forms, Cather's narration also involves other forms of everyday life practices. As has been partially discussed, dress and leisure activities are emblematic of Cather's new women figures and Thea's sojourn in Panther Canyon. Holiday celebrations and party goings portrayed in *My Ántonia*, *O Pioneers!*, *Death Comes for the Archbishop* and *Shadows on the Rock* are concerned with forms of daily practices which have gone beyond my proposed research and demand a further undertaking in the future studies. What I have done in this book is mainly based on Michel de Certeau's, Luce Giard's and Pierre Mayol's elaborations on different aspects of everyday life practices in the two volumes of *The Practice of Everyday Life*. Throughout this book, I find that Cather's literary imagination is filled with place and daily activities, such as cooking and storytelling that are gender-bound and ideologically interwoven. In her writings, Cather not only elevates these activities to the status of art, but also subverts the traditional associations between gender and cooking. In her writings, doing-cooking is not necessarily the duty of women, but can be taken over by men as well. Characters of this group include Peter in *My Ántonia*, who is quite fond of his cow and could "make butter by beating sour cream with a wooden spoon" (*NS* 734), the two bishops of *Death Comes for the Archbishop*, with Father Joseph being good at cooking and Bishop Latour being meticulous about gardening, and Old Henry in *The Professor's House*, who is a wonderful cook and a good housekeeper (*LN* 218).

Throughout this book, I approach Cather's everyday life from the angle of the practice of the neighborhood, doing-cooking and storytelling. The approach enables me to explore everyday life and fin de siècle literary imagination in Cather's works as has been shown in the discussion. Cather is such a writer whose achievement is uncontainable by labels of any kind. Straddling the late-Victorian and Modernist eras, Cather is a complex, transitional cultural figure whose sensibility is strongly forged by this shift. A detailed analysis of Cather's representation of everyday life in her major works reveals the resonances within her writing of the cultural formations of fin de siècle. She absorbs what her changing culture has offered to her and arises eventually from the circumambient cultural atmosphere of her particular historical moment. In her delineation of each detail of everyday life, readers witness her negotiations with the major changes of her age, her implicit critique of the costs of modernization and her endorsement of values represented by nineteenth century agrarian culture as well. Cather's aesthetics of everyday life is deeply rooted in the daily life, yet reaches far beyond one's usual life experiences. Everyday life details such as living and cooking do not simply document and illustrate what are explicitly stated; rather, one can extrapolate their political ramifications from them. In prioritizing and romanticizing the hard facts of everyday life in her major works, Cather manages to distill poetry out of the commonplace.

# Bibliography

[1] Abrams, M. H. *A Glossary of Literary Terms* (9th ed) [M]. Beijing: Foreign Language Teaching and Research Press, 2010.

[2] Acocella, J. *Willa Cather and the Politics of Criticism* [M]. Lincoln: The University of Nebraska Press, 2000.

[3] Ambrose, J. *Willa Cather Writing at the Frontier* [M]. New York: Berg Publishers Limited, 1988.

[4] Ammons, E. *Conflicting Stories: American Women Writers at the Turn into the Twentieth Century* [M]. Oxford: Oxford University Press, 1992.

[5] Arata, S. Realism [A]. The Cambridge Companion to the Fin de Siècle [C]. Cambridge: Cambridge University Press, 2007: 169-197.

[6] Arnold, M. *Willa Cather's Short Fiction* [M]. Athens, Ohio: Ohio University Press, 1984.

[7] Aron, C. S. *At Play: A History of Vacations in the United States* [M]. Oxford: Oxford University Press, 2001.

[8] Aronoff, E. Anthropologists, Indians, and New Critics: Culture and/as Poetic Form in Regional Modernism [J]. *Modern Fiction Studies*, 2009(55): 92-118.

[9] Baker, A. Terrible Women: Gender, Platonism, and Christianity in Willa Cather's *The Professor's House* [J]. *Western American Literature*, 2010, 45(3): 253-272.

[10] Bal, M. *Narratology: Introduction to the Theory of Narrative* [M]. Toronto: Toronto University Press, 1985.

[11] Barthes, R. Toward a Psychosociology of Contemporary Food Consumption [J]. *Counihan and Van Esterik*, 1961: 20-27.

[12] Beideck-Porn, L. R. A Celebration of Survival Secured: Food in the Narrative of Willa Cather [A]. Images of the Self as Female: The Achievement of Women Artists in Re-Envisioning Feminine Identity [C]. New York: Edwin Mellen, 1992: 213-223.

[13] Benfey, C. The Other Side of the Rug: Cather's Narrative Underpinnings [J]. *American Literary History*, 1994, 6(1): 140-154.

[14] Bennett, M. *The World of Willa Cather* [M]. Lincoln: The University of Nebraska Press, 1961.

[15] Bloom, E. A. The Genesis of *Death Comes for the Archbishop* [J]. *American Literature,* 1955, 24(4): 479-506.

[16] Bloom, L.D. *Willa Cather's Gift of Sympathy* [M].Carbondale: Southern Illinois University Press, 1962.

[17] Bloom, H. *Willa Cather: Bloom's Major Novelists* [M]. Broomall: Chelsea House Publishers, 2000.

[18] Boswell, M. and Rollyson, C. *Encyclopedia of American Literature 1607 to the Present* [M]. New York: Facts on File, Inc., 2002.

[19] Bourdieu, P. *Distinction: A Social Critique of the Judgment of Taste* [M]. London: Routledge and Kegan Paul, 1984.

[20] Brienzo G. *Willa Cather's Transforming Vision: New France and the American Northeast* [M]. Selinsgrove: Susquehanna University Press, 1994.

[21] Brodhead, R. H. *Cultures of Letters: Scenes of Reading and Writing in Nineteenth-Century America* [M]. Chicago: Chicago University Press, 1993.

[22] Broncano, M. Landscapes of the Magical: Cather's and Anaya's Explorations of the Southwest [A]. Willa Cather and the American Southwest [C]. Lincoln: The University of Nebraska Press, 2002: 124-135.

[23] Brown, E. K. and Edel, L. Willa Cather, A Critical Biography [C]. New York: Knopf, 1953.

[24] Brown, V. V. Willa Cather and the Southern Genteel Tradition [D]. Lubbock: Texas Tech University, 1989.

[25] Butcher, F. Willa Cather Called Leading Woman Writer—"Obscure Destinies" to Bring Her New Laurels [J]. *Chicago Daily Tribune*, 1932: 17.

[26] Camp, C. Review of Cather's Kitchens: Foodways in Literature and Life by Roger L. and Linda K. Welsch [J]. *Western Folklore,* 2002, 61(1): 111-112.

[27] Cao, Jinghua. *The Search for Female Identity—A Thematic Study of Willa Cather's Fictional Portrayal of Women* [M]. Beijing: The People's Liberation

Army Press, 1995.

[28] Carlin, D. *Cather, Canon, and the Politics of Reading* [M]. Amherst: Massachusetts University Press, 1992.

[29] Cather, W. *A Lost Lady* [M]. New York: Vintage Books, 1972.

[30] Cather, W. *The Bohemian Girl* [M]. New York: Harper Collins, 2009.

[31] Cather, W. *Death Comes for the Archbishop* [M]. New York: Vintage Books, 1971.

[32] Cather, W. *Early Novels and Stories* [M]. New York: Library of America, 1987.

[33] Cather, W. *The Kingdom of Art: Willa Cather's First Principles and Critical Statements 1893-1896* [M]. Lincoln: The University of Nebraska Press, 1966.

[34] Cather, W. *Later Novels* [M]. New York: Library of America, 1990.

[35] Cather, W. *One of Ours* [M]. New York: Alfred A. Knopf, 1922.

[36] Cather, W. *O Pioneers!* [M] San Diego: Icon Group International, Inc., 2005.

[37] Cather, W. *The Professor's House* [M]. New York: Vintage Books, 1990.

[38] Cather, W. *Sapphira and the Slave Girl* [M]. London: Cassell and Company, Ltd., 1941.

[39] Cather, W. *The Selected Letters of Willa Cather* [M]. New York: Alfred A. Knopf, 2013.

[40] Cather, W. *Stories, Poems, and Other Writings* [M]. New York: Library of America, 1992.

[41] Cather, W. Tommy, the Unsentimental [J]. *The Home Monthly,* 1896(8): 6-7.

[42] Cather, W. *Uncle Valentine and Other Stories: Willa Cather's Uncollected Short Fiction, 1915-1929* [M]. Lincoln: The University of Nebraska Press, 1973.

[43] Cather, W. *Willa Cather in Person: Interviews, Speeches and Letters* [M]. Lincoln: The University of Nebraska Press, 1986.

[44] Cather, W. *Willa Cather: Novels & Stories 1905-1918*[M]. New York: Library of America, 1999.

[45] Cather, W. *The World and the Parish: Willa Cather's Articles and Reviews, 1893-1902* [M]. Lincoln: The University of Nebraska Press, 1970.

[46] Chen, Miaoling. Ethical Analysis of Relationship between Human Beings and Land: Ecological Thoughts in Cather's *O Pioneers!* [J]. *Foreign Literature*

*Studies,* 2010(2): 126-134.

[47] Chinery, M. C. Carnival Tradition in Willa Cather's Fiction [D]. Madison: Drew University, 2003.

[48] Schedler, C. Modernist Borders of Our America: Intercultural Readings in American Literary Modernism [D]. Berkeley: California University, 1999.

[49] Clark, P. P. The Practice of Everyday Life by Michel de Certeau: Steven Rendall [J]. *The Journal of Modern History* 1986, 58(3): 705-707.

[50] Coulombe, J. L. *Mark Twain and the American West* [M]. Columbia: Missouri University Press, 2003.

[51] Cozzi, A. *The Discourse of Food in Nineteenth-century British Fiction* [M]. New York: Palgrave Macmillan, 2010.

[52] Daiches, D. *A Critical Introduction to Willa Cather* [M]. New York: Cornell University Press, 1962.

[53] Danker, K. A. The Passing of a Golden Age in *Obscure Destinies* [J]. *Willa Cather Pioneer Memorial Newsletter,* 1990(34): 24-28.

[54] De Certeau, M. *The Practice of Everyday Life* (Vol. I) [M]. Berkeley: California University Press, 1984.

[55] De Roche, L. *Student Companion to Willa Cather* [M]. Westport, Connecticut: Greenwood Press, 2006.

[56] Donovan, J. *New England Local Color Literature: Women's Tradition* [M]. New York: Ungar, 1983.

[57] Dooley, P. K. *Willa Cather's Ecological Imagination* [C]. Lincoln: The University of Nebraska Press, 2003: 65-76.

[58] Douglas, M. *Implicit Meanings: Essays in Anthropology* [M]. London: Routledge, 1975.

[59] Driedge, D. Writing Isolation and the Resistance to Assimilation as "Imaginative Art": Willa Cather's Anti-Narrative in Shadows on the Rock [J]. *Journal of Narrative Theory*, 2007, 37(3): 351-374.

[60] Dyck, R. Willa Cather's Reluctant New Woman Pioneer [J]. *Great Plains Quarterly,* 2013, 23(3): 161-173.

[61] Elahi, B. *The Fabric of American Literary Realism: Readymade Clothing, Social*

*Mobility and Assimilation* [M]. London: McFarland & Company, Inc., 2009.

[62] Elliott, E. Women Writers and the New Woman[A]. Columbia Literary History of the United States [C]. New York: Columbia University Press, 1988: 598-606.

[63] Ellwanger, A. On the Possibility of the Aesthetic Life: Terry Eagleton, Cather's Tom Outland, and the Experience of Loss [J]. *Journal of Modern Literature,* 2012, 35(2): 52-63.

[64] Epstein, A. Critiquing "La Vie Quotidienne": Contemporary Approaches to the Everyday [J]. *Contemporary Literature,* 2008, 49(3): 476-487.

[65] Fahy, T. *Freak Shows in Modern American Imagination: Constructing the Damaged Body from Willa Cather to Truman Capote* [M]. New York: Palgrave Macmillan, 2006.

[66] Fowler, R. *The Routledge Dictionary of Literary Terms* [M]. London: Routledge, 2006.

[67] Freedman, J. *Profession of Taste: Henry James, British Aestheticism, and Commodity Culture* [M]. Stanford, California: Stanford University Press, 1990.

[68] Fryer, J. *Felicitous Space: The Imaginative Structures of Edith Wharton and Willa Cather* [M]. Chapel Hill: The North Carolina University Press, 1986.

[69] Fuchs, M. O Madison! Drew University and Its Trove of Cather Papers [N]. *New York Times,* 2005-11-27(6).

[70] Funda, E. I. A Chorus of Gossips: Mistaking Invasion for Intimacy in Willa Cather's "A Lost Lady" [J]. *Narrative,* 1999, 7(1): 89-113.

[71] Funda, E. I. Every Word Counted for Twenty: Storytelling and Intimacy in Willa Cather's Fiction [D]. Lincoln: The University of Nebraska Press, 1994.

[72] Funda, E. I. Telling a Community's Story: The Epiphanies of Willa Cather's Shadows on the Rock. [J]. *Religion & Literature,* 1998, 31(1): 53-83.

[73] Gardiner, M. E. *Critiques of Everyday Life* [M]. New York: Routledge, 2000.

[74] Gelfant, B. The Forgotten Reaping-Hook: Sex in *My Ántonia* [J]. *American Literature,* 1971, 43(1): 60-82.

[75] Gerber, P. L. *Willa Cather* [M]. Boston: Twayne Publishers, 1975.

[76] Giard, L. and Mayol, P. *The Practice of Everyday Life* (Vol.II): *Living and Cooking* [M]. Minneapolis: Minnesota University Press, 1998.

[77] Giles, J. *The Parlour and the Suburb: Domestic Identities, Class, Femininity and Modernity* [M]. Oxford: Berg., 2004.

[78] Gillum, M. *Bloom's Literary Themes: The Grotesque* [M]. New York: Bloom's Literary Criticism Chelsea House Publications, 2009.

[79] Gilman, C. P. *Women and Economics: A Study of the Economic Relation Between Men and Women as a Factor in Social Evolution* [M]. Berkeley: California University Press, 1998.

[80] Gorman, M. Versed in Country Things: Pastoral Ideology, Modern American Identity, and Willa Cather [D]. Tulsa: The University of Tulsa. 2005.

[81] Gross, S. S. Antimodern strategies: Ambivalence, Accommodation, and Protest in Willa Cather's The Troll Garden [D]. Tulsa: University of Oklahoma, 2004.

[82] Halverson, C. *Playing House in the American West: Western Women's Life Narratives, 1839-1987* [M]. Tuscaloosa: Alabama University Press, 2013.

[83] Harpham, G. The Grotesque: First Principles [J]. *The Journal of Aesthetics and Art Criticism*, 1976, 34(4): 461-468.

[84] Harris, J. H. Les filles du roi and Female Destinations in Shadows on the Rock [J]. *Willa Cather Newsletter & Review*, 2010, 54(1): 16-21.

[85] Heller, T. and Moran, P. *Scenes of the Apple: Food and the Female Body in Nineteenth- and Twentieth-Century Women's Writing* [C]. Albany: State University of New York Press, 2003.

[86] Hellman, C. C. *Domesticity and Design in American Women's Lives and Literature: Stowe, Alcott, Cather and Wharton* [M]. New York: Routledge, 2011.

[87] Herron, S. Willa Cather's Argument with Modernism: Unearthing Faith amid the Ruins of War [D]. Newark: University of Delaware, 2007.

[88] Heyeck, R. and Woodress, J. Willa Cather's Cuts and Revisions in *The Song of the Lark* [J]. *Modern Fiction Studies*, 1979, 25(4): 651-658.

[89] Hicks, G. *Willa Cather and Her Critics* [C]. New York: Cornell University Press, 1967: 139-147.

[90] Highmore, B. *Everyday Life and Cultural Theory: An Introduction* [M]. New York: Routledge, 2002.

[91] Highmore, B. *The Everyday Life Reader* [M]. New York: Routledge, 2002.

[92] Hobby, B. *Bloom's Literary Themes: The Grotesque* [M]. New York: Bloom's Literary Criticism Chelsea House Publications, 2009.

[93] Homestead, M. J. and Reynolds, G. J. Willa Cather and Modern Cultures [C]. Lincoln: The University of Nebraska Press, 2011.

[94] Hoover, S. Willa Cather Remembered [C]. Lincoln: University of Nebraska Press, 2002.

[95] James, H. *The Bostonians* [M]. London: Macmillan, 1921.

[96] James, P. *The New Death: American Modernism and World War I* [M]. Charlottesville: University of Virginia Press, 2013.

[97] Jewell, A. A Crime against Art: *My Ántonia*, Food, and Cather's Anti-Americanization Argument [J]. *Willa Cather Newsletter & Review*, 2010, 54(2): 72-76.

[98] Tewell, A. Chocolate, Cannibalism, and Gastronomical Meaning in *Shadows on the Rock* [J]. Lincoln: The University of Nebraska Press, 2010: 282-294.

[99] Jewett, S. O. Letters of Sarah Orne Jewett [C]. Boston: Houghton, Mifflin & Co., 1911.

[100] Johanningsmeier, C. Willa Cather and the Nineteenth Century [C]. Lincoln: The University of Nebraska Press, 2015: 38-67.

[101] Tewell, A. The Making of "Die Tochter Der Prarie [Daughter of the Prairie]": Willa Cather's Fictions in Germany, 1926-1952 [J]. *Studies in the Novel,* 2013, 45(3): 559-579.

[102] Kaplan, W. *The Arts & Crafts Movement in Europe & America* [M]. New York: Thomas & Hudson in Association with the Los Angeles County Museum of Art, 2004.

[103] Kaufman, A. L. and Millington, R. H. Willa Cather and the Nineteenth Century [C]. Lincoln: The University of Nebraska Press, 2015.

[104] Keeler, C. Narrative without Accent: Willa Cather and Puvis de Chavannes [J]. *American Quarterly*, 1965, 17(1): 119-126.

[105] Kohler, A. New Woman Hybridities: Femininity, Feminism and International Consumer Culture, 1880-1930 [C]. London: Routledge, 2004.

[106] Lachmann, R. , Eshelman, R. and Davis M. Bakhtin and Carnival: Culture as Counter-Culture [J]. *Cultural Critique,* 1998, (11): 115-152.

[107] Langer, B. *The Practice of Everyday Life* by Michel de Certeau [J]. *Contemporary Sociology*, 1988, 17(1): 122-124.

[108] Leder, P. Digesting the Male Tradition: Food and Drink in *The Song of the Lark* [J]. *Willa Cather Newsletter & Review*, 2010, 54(2): 56-59.

[109] Ledger, S. *The New Woman: Fiction and Feminism at the Fin de Siècle* [M]. Manchester: Manchester University Press, 1997.

[110] Lee, H. Willa Cather: A Hidden Voice [J]. *The New York Review of Books*, 2013, 60(12): 46.

[111] Lee, H. *Willa Cather: Double Lives* [M]. New York: Vintage, 1989.

[112] Lefebvre, H. *Critique of Everyday Life: Introduction* [M]. London: Verso, 2008.

[113] Lefebvre, H. *Critique of Everyday Life* [M]. London: Verso, 2002.

[114] Lefebvre, H. *Everyday Life in the Modern World* [M]. New York: The Penguin Press, 1971.

[115] Levine, L. W. *Highbrow/Lowbrow: The Emergence of Cultural Hierarchy in America* [M]. Cambridge: Harvard University Press, 1988.

[116] Levy, H. F. *Fiction of the Home Place: Jewett, Cather, Glasgow, Porter, Welty, and Naylor* [M]. Jackson: University of Mississippi Press, 1992.

[117] Lewis, E. *Willa Cather Living: A Personal Record* [M]. New York: Octagon Books, 1976.

[118] Li, Li. *A Study of Willa Cather's Memory Writing* [M]. Chengdu: Sichuan University Press, 2009.

[119] Lopez, E. M. The Pursuit of Property: Race and Identity in American Fiction, 1885-1948 [D]. Rochester: The University of Rochester, 2004.

[120] Lu, Xingren. Approaching the Feminist Daily Life Poetics—Discussion on the Meaning of Daily Life in Feminist Criticism [D]. Wuhan: Central China Normal University, 2007.

[121] Lucenti, L. M. Willa Cather's *My Ántonia*: Haunting the Houses of Memory [J]. *Twentieth Century Literature*, 2000, 46(2):193-213.

[122] Lynch, S. F. and Lynch, R. L. Willa Cather and Aestheticism [C]. Madison:

Fairleigh Dickinson University Press, 2012: 29-40.

[123] Mabie, H. W. A Typical Novel [J]. *Andover Review*, 1885(4): 419-429.

[124] Macleod, K. Art for America's Sake: Decadence and the Making of American Literary Culture in the Little Magazines of the 1890s [J]. *Prospects*, 2005, 30: 309-338.

[125] Mangum, T. *Married, Middlebrow, and Militant: Sarah Grand and the New Woman Novel* [M]. Ann Arbor: University of Michigan Press, 1999.

[126] Marks, P. *Bicycles, Bangs, and Bloomers* [M]. Lexington: University Press of Kentucky, 1990.

[127] Marshall, G. *The Cambridge Companion to the Fin de Siècle* [M]. Cambridge: Cambridge University Press, 2007.

[128] Martin, E. *The Practice of Everyday Life, Volume 2: Living & Cooking* by Michel de Certeau; Luce Giard; Pierre Mayol; Timonthy J. Tomasik [J]. *Symploke*, 1999, 7(1): 208-210.

[129] McDonald, J. *The Stuff of Our Forebears: Willa Cather's Southern Heritage* [M]. Tuscaloosa: The University of Alabama Press, 1998.

[130] McKenzie, M. M. Willa Cather's Southern Connections: New Essays on Cather and the South [C]. Charlottesville: The University of Virginia, 2000: 83-89.

[131] Meyering, S. L. *A Reader's Guide to the Short Stories of Willa Cather* [M]. New York: G. K. Hall, 1994.

[132] Middleton, J. A. *Willa Cather's Modernism: A Study of Style and Technique* [M]. Rutherford: Fairleigh Dickinson University Press, 1990.

[133] Millington, R. H. Cather Studies 4: Willa Cather's Canadian and Old World Connections [C]. Lincoln: The University of Nebraska Press, 1999: 23-44.

[134] Millington, R. H. Willa Cather and "The Storyteller": Hostility to the Novel in *My Ántonia* [J]. 1994,66(4): 689-717.

[135] Millington, R. H. The Cambridge Companion to Willa Cather [C]. Cambridge: Cambridge University Press, 2005: 51-65.

[136] Molino, M. R. *The Oxford Encyclopedia of British Literature* [M]. Shanghai: Shanghai Foreign Language Education Press, 2011: 98-102.

[137] Morley, C. Crossing the Water: Willa Cather and the Transatlantic Imaginary

[J]. *European Journal of American Culture*, 2009, 28(2): 125-140.

[138] Morris, W. *The Beauty of Life* [M]. London: Longmans Green and Company, 1881.

[139] Morrison, T. *Playing in the Dark: Whiteness and the Literary Imagination* [M]. Cambridge: Harvard University Press, 1992.

[140] Murphy, J. J. *Critical Essays on Willa Cather* [M]. Boston: G. K. Hall & Co., 1984.

[141] Murphy, J. J. *Influencing America's Taste: Realism in the Works of Wharton, Cather, and Hurst* by Stephanie Lewis Thompson [J]. *American Literary Realism*, 2003, 35(3): 270-271.

[142] Murphy, J. J and Skaggs, M. M. Willa Cather: New Facts, New Glimpse, Revisions [C]. Madison: Fairleigh Dickinson University Press, 2008.

[143] Nelson, R. J. *Willa Cather and the France: In Search of the Lost Language* [M]. Chicago: The University of Illinois Press, 1988.

[144] Nettles, E. Wharton and Cather [J]. *American Literary Scholarship*, 2000:123-138.

[145] Nettles, E. Wharton and Cather [J]. *American Literary Scholarship*, 2002: 119-135.

[146] Oates, J. C. *Haunted: Tales of the Grotesque* [M]. New York: Plume Press, 1994.

[147] O'Brien, S. *Felicitous Space: The Imaginative Structures of Edith Wharton and Willa Cather* by Judith Fryer; *The Voyage Perilous: Willa Cather's Romanticism* by Susan J. Rosowski [J]. *Contemporary Literature*, 1988, 29(1): 125-128.

[148] O'Brien, S. American Novelists Revisited: Essays in Feminist Criticism [C]. Boston: G. K. Hall, 1982: 265-298.

[149] O'Brien, S. *Willa Cather: The Emerging Voice* [M]. New York: Oxford University Press, 1987.

[150] O'Brien, S. New Essays on My Ántonia [C]. Beijing: Peking University Press, 2007.

[151] O'Connor, M. A. Willa Cather: The Contemporary Reviews [C]. Cambridge:

Cambridge University Press, 2001.

[152] Olson, L. Everyday Life Studies: A Review [J]. *Modernism/Modernity,* 2011, 18(1): 175-180.

[153] Parkins, W. William Morris and the Art of Everyday Life [C]. Newcastle: Cambridge Scholars Publishing, 2010.

[154] Parrish, T. The Cambridge Companion to American Novelists [C]. Cambridge: Cambridge University Press, 2013.

[155] Pattee, F. L. *The New American Literature, 1890-1930* [M]. New York: Appleton-Century Company Incorporated, 1937.

[156] Patterson, M. H. *Beyond the Gibson Girl: Reimagining the American New Woman, 1895-1915* [M]. Urbana: University of Illinois Press, 2005.

[157] Peck, D. C. *The Imaginative Claims of the Artist in Willa Cather's Fiction* [M]. London: Associated University Press, 1996.

[158] Petrie, P. R. "Skulking Escapist" Versus 'Radical Editor': Willa Cather, the Left Critics and Sapphira and the Slave Girl [J]. *Southern Quarterly*, 1996, 34(2): 27-37.

[159] Petrie, P. R. "There Must be Something Wonderful Coming": Social Purpose and Romantic Idealism in Willa Cather's "Behind the Singer Tower" [J]. *American Literary Realism,* 2001, 33(2): 110-122.

[160] Piatti-Farnell, L. *Food and Culture in Contemporary American Fiction* [M]. New York: Routledge, 2011.

[161] Pogue, L. B. L. Devouring Words: Eating and Feeding in Selected Fiction of Kate Chopin, Edith Wharton, and Willa Cather [D]. Waco: Baylor University, 2000.

[162] Pratt, A. The New Feminist Criticism [J]. *College English,*1971,(32): 872-878.

[163] Prenatt, D. Cather Studies 9: Willa Cather and Modern Cultures [C]. Lincoln: The University of Nebraska Press, 2011: 204-224.

[164] Pykett, L. *The "Improper Feminine": The Women's Sensation Novel and the New Woman Writing* [M]. London: Routledge, 1992.

[165] Quantic, D. D. The Open Window: Domestic Landscapes in Willa Cather's *My Ántonia* and *Sapphira and the Slave Girl* [J]. *American Studies*, 2002, 43(2):

103-122.

[166] Quirk, T. In *Alexander's Bridge* by Willa Cather [C]. Lincoln: The University of Nebraska Press.

[167] Quirk, T. and Scharnhornst, G. American History through Literature, 1870-1920 [C]. Detroit: Thomson Gale, 2006.

[168] Rabin G. J. *Surviving the Crossing (Im)migration, Ethnicity and Gender in Willa Cather, Gertrude Stein and Nella Larsen* [M]. New York: Routledge, 2004.

[169] Railton, B. Research Guide to American Literature: American Modernism 1914-1945 [C]. New York: Facts on File, Inc., 2010:108-113.

[170] Randall, B. *Modernism, Daily Time, and Everyday Life* [M]. Cambridge: Cambridge University Press, 2008.

[171] Randall, J. H. *The Landscape and the Looking Glass: Willa Cather's Search for Value* [M]. Boston: Houghton Mifflin, 1960.

[172] Randall, J. H. Critical Essays on Willa Cather [C]. Boston: G. K. Hall & Co., 1984: 247-251.

[173] Rapin, R. *Willa Cather* [M]. New York: R. M. McBride Co., 1930.

[174] Reynolds, G. The Transatlantic Virtual Salon: Cather and the British [J]. *Studies in the Novel*, 2013,45(3): 349-368.

[175] Reynolds, G. *Willa Cather in Context: Progress, Race, Empire* [M]. New York: St. Martin's, 1996.

[176] Richardson, A. and Wills, C. *The New Woman in Fiction and in Fact: Fin-de-siècle Feminisms* [M]. New York: Palgrave, 2001.

[177] Robinson, M. A. Making a Career of Play: Willa Cather and the Recreational Movement [D]. Lincoln: The University of Nebraska Press, 2008.

[178] Rogal, S. J. *From Whom the Bell Tolls: The Role and Function of Food and Drink in the Prose of Ernest Hemingway* [M]. San Francisco: International Scholars, 1997.

[179] Romines, A. *At Willa Cather's Tables: The Cather Foundation Cookbook* [M]. Lincoln: Willa Cather Foundation, 2010.

[180] Romines, A. "Historical Essay" and "Explanatory Notes" of *Sapphira and the*

Slave Girl [C]. Lincoln: The University of Nebraska Press, 2009.

[181] Romines, A. *The Home Plot: Women, Writing & Domestic Ritual* [M]. Amherst: The University of Massachusetts Press, 1992.

[182] Romines, A. Willa Cather and "the Old Story": *Sapphira and the Slave Girl* [A]. The Cambridge Companion to Willa Cather [C]. Cambridge: Cambridge University Press, 2005: 205-221.

[183] Romines, A. Food and Drink and the Art of Willa Cather [J]. *The Willa Cather Newsletter & Review,* 2010, 54(2): 30-91.

[184] Rosowski, S. J. After the Christmas Tree: Willa Cather and Domestic Ritual [J]. *American Literature*, 1988, 60(1): 61-82.

[185] Rosowski, S. J. Introduction: Willa Cather and American Literary Realism [J]. *American Literary Realism*, 2001, 33(2): 95-98.

[186] Rosowski, S. J. *The Voyage Perilous: Willa Cather's Romanticism* [M]. Lincoln: The University of Nebraska Press, 1986.

[187] Rosowski, S. J. *The Oxford Encyclopedia of American Literature* [M]. Shanghai: Shanghai Foreign Language Education Press, 2011: 240-250.

[188] Rosowski, S. J. Prospects for the Study of American Literature: A Guide for Scholars and Students [C]. New York: New York University Press, 1997: 219-240.

[189] Rosowski, S. J. Willa Cather's *A Lost Lady*: The Paradoxes of Change [J]. *Novel: A Forum on Fiction*, 1977(11): 51-62.

[190] Rosowski, S. J. Willa Cather's Subrerted Endings and Gendered Time [A] Cather Studies 1[C]. Lincoln: The University of Nebraska Press, 1990: 68-88.

[191] Rothman, H. *Devil's Bargains: Tourism in the Twentieth-Century American West* [M]. Lawrence: University Press of Kansas, 2000.

[192] Ryder, M. R. Such News of the Land: U. S. Women Nature Writers [C]. Hanover: University Press of New England, 2001.

[193] Scharnhorst, G.Willa Cather [J]. *American Literary Realism*, 2001, 33(2): 95-187.

[194] Schedler, C. *Border Modernism* [M]. New York: Routledge, 2002.

[195] Schilling, D. Everyday Life and the Challenge to History in Postwar France:

Braudel, Lefebvre, Certeau [J]. *Diacritics*, 2003, 33(1): 23-40.

[196] Schor, N. Cartes Postales: Representing Paris 1900 [J]. *Critical Inquiry*, 1992(18): 188-241.

[197] Schroeter, J. *Willa Cather and Her Critics* [M]. Ithaca: Cornell University Press, 1967.

[198] Sergeant, E. S. *Willa Cather: A Memoir* [M]. Lincoln: The University of Nebraska Press, 1963.

[199] Shaw, P. W. *Willa Cather and the Art of Conflict: Re-Visioning Her Creative Imagination* [M]. New York: The Whitston Publishing Company, 1992.

[200] Sheringham, M. *Everyday Life Theories and Practices: from Surrealism to the Present* [M]. Oxford: Oxford University Press, 2006.

[201] Shimotakahara, L. Regional Modernism: The Vanishing Landscape in American Literature and Culture, 1896-1952 [D]. Providence: Brown University, 2007.

[202] Shively, S. B. Driven by Starvation: Hunger in Cather's *Death Comes for the Archbishop* and *Shadows on the Rock* [J]. *Willa Cather Newsletter & Review*, 2010, 54(2): 81-84.

[203] Singley, C. J. and Moseley, A. Wharton and Cather [J]. *American Literary Scholarship*, 2004: 127-149.

[204] Skaggs, M. M. Willa Cather: A Literary Life by James Woodress [J]. *American Literature*, 1988, 60(3): 493-495.

[205] Skaggs, M. M. *After the World Broke in Two: The Later Novels of Willa Cather* [M]. Charlottesville: University Press of Virginia, 1990.

[206] Skaggs, M. M. *Willa Cather's New York: New Essays on Cather in the City* [C]. Teaneck: Fairleigh Dickinson University Press, 2000.

[207] Slocum, J. *Lucy Gayheart* by Willa Cather [J]. *The North American Review*, 1935, 240(3): 549-550.

[208] Slote, B. *Fifteen Modern American Authors: A Survey of Research and Criticism* [C]. Durham: Duke University Press, 1969.

[209] Slocum, J. *Willa Cather: A Pictorial Memoir* [M]. Lincoln: The University of Nebraska Press, 1986.

[210] Smith, E. Of Coconut Cake and Consomme: Willa Cather's School of Cookery

[J]. *Willa Cather Newsletter & Review*, 54 (2): 77-80.

[211] Smith-Rosenberg, C. *Disorderly Conduct: Visions of Gender in Victorian America* [M]. Oxford: Oxford University Press, 1985.

[212] Spindler, M. Thorstein Veblen and Modern American Fiction [J]. *Australasian Journal of American Studies*, 1992(11): 37-50.

[213] Stouck, D. "Historical Essay" and "Explanatory Notes" of *O Pioneers!* [C]. Lincoln: The University of Nebraska Press, 1992: 283-348.

[214] Stouck, D. Willa Cather's Last Four Books [C]. Boston: G. K. Hall, 1984: 290-304.

[215] Stout, J. P. Dorothy Canfield, Willa Cather, and the Uncertainties of Middlebrow and Highbrow [J]. *Studies in the Novel*, 2012, 44(1): 27-48.

[216] Stout, J. P. *Picturing a Different West: Vision, Illustration, and the Tradition of Cather and Austin* [M]. Lubbock: Texas Tech University Press, 2007.

[217] Stout, J. P. Seeing and Believing: Willa Cather's Realism [J]. *American Literary Realism,* 2001(33): 168-180.

[218] Stout, J. P. *Willa Cather: The Writer and Her World* [M]. Charlottesville: University Press of Virginia, 2000.

[219] Stout, J. P. A Calendar of the Letters of Willa Cather [C]. Lincoln: The University of Nebraska Press, 2002.

[220] Stout, J. P. Willa Cather and Material Culture: Real-World Writing, Writing the Real World [C]. Tuscaloosa: The University of Alabama Press, 2005.

[221] Summers, C. J. A Losing Game in the End: Aestheticism and Homosexuality in Cather's "Paul's Case" [J]. *Modern Fiction Studies*, 1990, 36(1): 103-119.

[222] Sun, Hong. The Ghost in the Machine: The Multicultural Complex in Willa Cather's Fiction [J]. *Foreign Literature Studies*,2007(5): 58-66.

[223] Sun, Hong. The Sense of the Biotic Community Encoded in Willa Cather's Works [J]. *Foreign Literature Studies*, 2009(2): 71-80.

[224] Sun, Ling. A Study of Willa Cather's Novels from the Perspective of Ecofeminist Literary Criticism [D]. Changchun: Jilin University, 2012.

[225] Swift, C. C. and Swift, J. N. Willa Cather and American Plant Ecology [J]. *Interdisciplinary Studies in Literature and Environment*, 2001, 8(2): 1-12.

[226] Swift, J. N. and Urgo, J. R. Willa Cather and the American Southwest [C]. Lincoln: The University of Nebraska Press, 2002.

[227] Tan, Jinghua. *Willa Cather's Ecological Vision* [M]. Beijing: Beijing Normal University Press, 2011.

[228] Thacker, R. It's through Myself that I Knew and Felt Her: S. S. McClure's "My Autobiography" and the Development of Willa Cather's Autobiographical Realism [J]. *American Literary Realism*, 2001, 33(2): 123-142.

[229] Thayer, W. R. The New Story-Tellers and the Doom of Realism [J]. *Forum*, 1894(18): 470-480.

[230] Thomas, S. *Willa Cather* [C]. London: Macmillan Education Ltd., 1990.

[231] Thompson, S. L. *Influencing America's Tastes—Realism in the Works of Wharton, Cather and Hurst* [M]. Gainesville: University Press of Florida, 2002.

[232] Tomasik, T. J. Certeau a la Carte—Translating Discursive Terroir in *The Practice of Everyday Life: Living and Cooking* [J]. *The South Atlantic Quarterly*, 2001, 100(2): 519-542.

[233] Trilling, L. Women Writers of The Short Story: A Collection of Critical Essay [C]. Englewood Cliffs: Printice-Hall, In., 1980: 61-68.

[234] Trout, S. Cather Studies 7: Willa Cather as Cultural Icon [C]. Lincoln: The University of Nebraska Press, 2007: 269-287.

[235] Trout, S. Encyclopedia of American Literature 1607 to the Present [C]. New York: Facts on File, Inc: 220-223.

[236] Trout, S. Cather Studies 6: History, Memory, and War [C]. Lincoln: The University of Nebraska Press, 2006.

[237] Urgo, J. R. *Willa Cather and the Myth of American Migration* [M]. Urbana: The University of Illinois Press, 1995.

[238] Urgo, J. R. and Skaggs, M. M. Violence, the Arts and Willa Cather [C]. Teaneck: Fairleigh Dickinson University Press, 2007.

[239] Veblen, T. *The Theory of the Leisure Class* [M]. Oxford: Oxford University Press, 2007.

[240] Wagenknecht, E. *Willa Cather* [M]. New York: The Continuum Publishing Company, 1994.

[241] Wall, A. and Thomson, C. Cleaning up Bakhtin's Carnival Act [J]. *Diacritics*, 1993, 23(2): 47-70.

[242] Warner, C. D. Modern Fiction [J]. *Aesthetic Monthly*, 1883(51): 464-474.

[243] Wasserman, L. Alexander's Bridge: The Other First Novel [D]. Lincoln: The University of Nebraska Press, 1999: 294-306.

[244] Wasserman, L. *Willa Cather: A Study of the Short Fiction* [M]. Boston: Twayne Publishers, 1991.

[245] Watson, S. C. Servant of Beauty: Willa Cather and the Aesthetic Movement [D]. College Station: Texas A & M University, 1999.

[246] Watson, S. C. and Moseley, A. Willa Cather and Aestheticism: From Romanticism to Modernism [C]. Teaneck: Fairleigh Dickinson University Press, 2013.

[247] Wegner, P. E. Introducing Criticism at the 21st Century [C]. Qingdao: Ocean University Press, 2006:179-201.

[248] Welsch, R. L. and Welsch, L. K. *Cather's Kitchens: Foodways in Literature and Life* [M]. Lincoln: The University of Nebraska Press, 1987.

[249] Wilde, O. The Artist as Critic: Critical Writings of Oscar Wilde [C]. Chicago: The University of Chicago Press, 1969: 290-320.

[250] Williams, D. L. Willa Cather and Material Culture: Real-World Writing, Writing the Real World [C]. Tuscaloosa: The University of Alabama Press, 2005: 156-170.

[251] Wilson, E. *The Shores of Light: A Literary Chronicle of the Twenties and Thirties* [M]. New York: The Noonday Press, 1952.

[252] Woodress, J. The Genesis of the Prologue of *Death Comes for the Archbishop* [J]. *American Literature*, 1978, 50(3): 473-478.

[253] Woodress, J. *Willa Cather: A Literary Life* [M]. Lincoln: The University of Nebraska Press, 1987.

[254] Xu,Yan. Tragedies and Achievements of Americanization in *O Pioneers!* [J]. *Foreign Literatures*, 2011(4):133-141.

[255] Yang, Haiyan. *Red Cloud Revisited: An Ecofeminist Study of Willa Cather* [M]. Chengdu: Sichuan University Press, 2006.

[256] Zabel, M. D. Willa Cather [J]. *Nation*, 1947(164): 713-716.

[257] Zhou, Ming. Good Citizen's Asylum—National Identification in the Progressive Era Represented in *My Ántonia* [J]. *Foreign Literature Review*, 2012(3): 65-86.

[258] Zhou, Ming. *Toward A Humanistic Spatial Poetics—A Study of Willa Cather's Major Novels* [M]. Beijing: Renmin University of China Press, 2009.

[259] Zhu, Li. Race, Place and Language: The Southern Idiom in *Sapphira and the Slave Girl* [J]. *Willa Cather Pioneer Memorial Newsletter*, 1998, 41(3): 72-75.